Benefits, Costs, and Finance of Public Higher Education

W. LEE HANSEN and
BURTON A. WEISBROD
University of Wisconsin

Markham Series in Public Policy Analysis

MARKHAM PUBLISHING COMPANY
Chicago

MARKHAM SERIES IN PUBLIC POLICY ANALYSIS

Julius Margolis and Aaron Wildavsky, Editors

Bogart, ed., *Social Research and the Desegregation of the U.S. Army*

Davis and Dolbeare, *Little Groups of Neighbors: The Selective Service System*

Feldstein, *Economic Analysis for Health Service Efficiency*

Hansen and Weisbrod, *Benefits, Costs, and Finance of Public Higher Education*

To T. W. Schultz

PREFACE

This is a study of the methodology for estimating the benefits and costs of higher education for a state, and of the relationship of these benefits and costs to legislative policy. The original study was commissioned in September of 1967 by the Joint Committee on Higher Education, established by the California State Legislature in 1965. The present volume is a revision of the original study and includes an additional section (Epilogue) on financing higher education.

The study adopts a broad benefit-cost framework for examining a variety of issues concerning higher education, with particular reference to the state of California. Specifically, it seeks to identify, classify, and measure the economic and social benefits and costs associated with higher education, to present an agenda for future quantitative research, and to set forth a framework for relating benefits and costs to such legislative policy issues as the appropriate level and sources of support for higher education. Although our emphasis is on California, we believe that the methodology and, to a significant degree, the quantitative estimates, are applicable more generally.

We have not attempted to propose specific solutions to the complex of problems involving the manner in which a state's higher education system should be organized, operated, and financed. Rather, we have tried to specify the kinds of considerations and information that are germane to finding those solutions. In so doing we emphasize that individual judgments about equity should enter the decision-making process, but so also should considerations of efficiency.

We wish to emphasize that much of the empirical work is illustrative rather than definitive. Because of great gaps in the data on all aspects of higher education and the quality of some of the data which do exist, we have been forced in many cases to make our own estimates, relying upon various published or unpublished studies and reports, and on the educated guesses of knowledgeable experts.

Finally, we note that little effort has been made to relate the large volume of already published work on the economics of higher education to the material presented here. While some references are presented, the interested reader is advised to consult some of the standard bibliographies for additional references.

We particularly want to thank Martha Strayhorn and Peter Karpoff for their substantial contributions to the research effort. We also wish to thank Felicity Skidmore, Richard Bailey, and the late John Melder for their assistance. The secretarial work was ably managed by Sharon Schlough and assisted by Daphne McDaniel.

In preparing the original report, the staff of the Joint Committee on Higher Education, notably Sherry L. Bebitch and Jerome Evans, provided invaluable advice and effective liaison with a variety of state agencies and departments. A number of people assisted us in obtaining and interpreting the available data. Included were officials from the California Office of the Legislative Analyst, Department of Finance, Department of Education, University of California, California State Colleges, Coordinating Council for Higher Education, State Scholarship and Loan Commission, and College Entrance Examination Board.

Also, we wish to acknowledge the useful suggestions by Jesse Burkhead, Alfred W. Baxter, our colleagues in the Department of Economics and the Department of Educational Policy Studies, and our students in the Workshop of the Economics of Human Resources.

In undertaking this study we were given complete freedom to explore whatever issues seemed to us to be significant and to investigate them in an objective and scholarly way. The results are our responsibility, and they reflect our views alone.

Madison, Wisconsin   W.L.H.
December, 1968   B.A.W.

CONTENTS

LIST OF TABLES

CHAPTER III

CHAPTER IV

INTRODUCTION[1]

The continued growth in college enrollments and in the number of college educated people reflects increasingly the view that college attendance is and should be a part of the normal educational experience of young people in our society today. Not only has the demand for college educated persons expanded very rapidly, as reflected by the large financial returns to people with college degrees, but at the same time there has developed a widespread belief that higher education offers a large and abundant source of other returns that redound to society at large. As a consequence, a sharply increasing fraction of both private and public resources is being devoted to expenditures on higher education.

While the private and social benefits of higher education may be substantial, these benefits are not attained without cost. Individuals must make sizable out-of-pocket expenditures to attend college; in addition, their incomes are greatly reduced during the period of college attendance. At the same time, society must divert a portion of its resources to providing general financial support for higher education. In view of increases in these support costs, concern has mounted in recent years—at the state as well as at the national level—about whether the upward trend of public support should be permitted to continue at its current pace and whether the current distribution of support should continue unchanged.

These concerns reflect the development of several forces. First, as a result of the post-World War II baby boom, the number of young people of college age has increased dramatically in the past

[1] If further reading is desired, *Economics of Education: A Selected Annotated Bibliography* (New York: Pergamon Press, 1966), edited by Mark Blaug, provides an excellent selection.

decade. Thus, the public support required simply to make available the same amount of higher education as before to the same proportion of college age people has had to be increased markedly. Second, although the fraction of high school graduates desiring to acquire college training has held relatively constant at around 50 percent, the proportion of young people graduating from high school has continued to increase, thereby giving rise to even greater financial needs for higher education. Third, these financial pressures have been further accentuated by the increasing fraction of all college students enrolled in upper division and graduate programs, where the cost per student is substantially greater than at the undergraduate level. Finally, there have been growing demands to make higher education available to qualified students who do not possess sufficient financial resources to attend college.

Against this background, state and local governments—which provide the major public support for higher education—also have been under sharp pressure to increase budgetary allocations for the whole gamut of other social services. This has placed tremendous pressure on the state and local tax base. As part of the process of adjustment to these pressures, the rate of increase in expenditures per student in higher education has been falling in recent years, resulting in a rise in student-faculty ratios. All of this has led to great concern at the state level about the problems of resource allocation in general and about the problems of resource allocation in higher education in particular.

In any consideration of the wide range of issues in the economics of higher education, perspective is gained by knowing whether some of the developing trends of the past decade can be expected to continue, to become magnified, or to lessen. The accompanying tables provide some indication of these trends.

1. The proportion of the college age population (age 18–21) will continue to rise until 1975, although the total numbers of persons in that age class will continue to increase until at least 1980 (Table 1).

2. Of this rising proportion of college age population, a rising fraction is expected to be enrolled in college. This means continuing increases in college enrollments, even though the rate of increase will be slightly slower than over the past decade (Table 2).

TABLE 1. REPORTED AND PROJECTED TOTAL POPULATION
AND COLLEGE AGE POPULATION (AGE 18–21), U.S.,
1955–1980

Year	Total Population (Millions)	Age 18–21 (Millions)	Percentage Age 18–21
1955	165.9	8.5	5.1%
1960	180.7	9.7	5.4
1965	194.6	12.3	6.3
1970	207.3	14.5	7.0
1975	223.8	16.3	7.3
1980	243.2	17.1	7.0

Sources: Column 1: U.S. Department of Commerce, Bureau of the Census, *Current Population Reports*, Series P–25, Nos. 321, 352, 359. Column 2: U.S. Department of Health, Education, and Welfare, Office of Education, *Projections of Educational Statistics to 1975–76* (1966 ed.), Table E, p. 102.

3. Based on national projections, not only will there be more students but they will be staying in school longer than ever before. These data indicate that the numbers of students graduating from college will increase faster than the numbers of persons with only one to three years of college. Meanwhile, the numbers with post-graduate work will rise more

TABLE 2. REPORTED AND PROJECTED COLLEGE AGE
POPULATION (AGE 18–21) AND HIGHER EDUCATION
DEGREE CREDIT ENROLLMENT, U.S., 1955–1980

Year	College Age Population (Millions)	Higher Education Degree Credit Enrollment (Millions)	Percentage Enrolled
1955	8.5	2.7	32%
1960	9.7	3.6	37
1965	12.3	5.5	45
1970	14.5	7.3	50
1975	16.3	9.0	55
1980	17.1	N.A.*	N.A.*

Sources: Column 1: U.S. Department of Health, Education, and Welfare, Office of Education, *Projections of Educational Statistics to 1975–76*, Table E, p. 102. Column 2: *Ibid.*, Table 4, p. 9.

* Data not available.

TABLE 3. YEARS OF HIGHER EDUCATION COMPLETED, FOR PERSONS AGE 25 AND OVER, 1960, AND PROJECTIONS TO 1985, U.S.

	(1) 1-3 Years of College		(2) 4 Years of College		(3) 5 or More Years of College		Total (1) + (2) + (3)	
	No. of Persons	Percentage of Total	No. of Persons	Percentage of Total	No. of Persons	Percentage of Total	No. of Persons	Percentage of Total
1960								
All persons*	8,742	54%	4,613	28%	3,012	18%	16,367	100%
Males*	4,123	47	2,510	29	2,129	24	8,762	100
Females*	4,619	61	2,103	28	883	11	7,605	100
1965								
All	9,706	51	5,637	30	3,520	19	18,863	100
Males	4,595	45	3,094	30	2,595	25	10,284	100
Females	5,111	59	2,543	30	926	11	8,580	100
1970								
All	10,961	50	7,008	31	4,195	19	22,164	100
Males	5,181	42	3,892	32	3,156	26	12,229	100
Females	5,780	58	3,116	31	1,039	11	9,935	100
1975								
All	12,723	48	8,794	33	5,083	19	26,600	100
Males	6,033	41	4,928	33	3,887	26	14,848	100
Females	6,690	57	3,866	33	1,196	10	11,752	100
1980								
All	14,797	47	10,847	34	6,140	19	31,784	100
Males	7,040	40	6,126	34	4,736	26	17,902	100
Females	7,757	56	4,721	34	1,404	10	13,882	100

Source: *Projections of Educational Attainment in the United States: 1965 to 1985* (Washington, D.C.: U.S. Dept. of Commerce, Series P-25, No. 305, April 14, 1965), pp. 7-10.
* All entries refer to persons age 25 years and over.

rapidly than the numbers of bachelor degree holders. Thus, the pressures on public support will continue to mount (Table 3).

4. Over the past decade, there has been a sharp rise in public expenditures for institutions of higher education; in addition, these expenditures constitute a rapidly growing fraction of all state and local government expenditures. Although federal expenditures on higher education have been increasing, they have not yet had an appreciable effect in lightening the burden of state and local governments (Table 4).

TABLE 4. STATE AND LOCAL AND TOTAL GOVERNMENTAL EXPENDITURES FOR INSTITUTIONS FOR HIGHER EDUCATION, 1955–1965

Year	State and Local Expenditures on Higher Education (Billions)	Higher Education Expenditures as Percentage of Total State and Local Expenditures	All Government Expenditures on Higher Education (Billions)	Higher Education Expenditures as Percentage of Total Governmental Expenditures
1955	$1.6	4.0%	$1.6	2.9%
1960	3.2	5.3	3.2	3.9
1965	5.9	6.8	5.9	5.0

Sources: Column 1: U.S. Bureau of the Census, *Statistical Abstract* (1967), Table 588, p. 423. Column 3: *Ibid.*, Table 585, p. 421.

Several interesting conclusions can be drawn from these data. First, demographic factors will cause continued growth in higher education enrollments during the coming decade. Second, this growth will be magnified by the increasing proportions of young people attending college and by the increase in the length of time they will be in college. For these reasons, the rapid growth of total public expenditures and particularly public expenditures for higher education is not likely to slow appreciably, if at all, during the coming decade.

Society's efforts to cope with policy for financing higher education have been stop-gap in nature—with no resolution of the basic issue as to who should pay. The provision of public funds has been influenced by the customary view that higher education is a good thing, so that whatever resources are required should be provided within reason. Increasingly, however, people are inquiring as to the nature and magnitude of the benefits provided by higher education. Questions of this sort arise naturally, but the increased emphasis being placed upon program budgeting and cost-benefit analysis in the evaluation of all kinds of public expenditure programs will put higher education under wider and more searching scrutiny. At the same time, with the growing emphasis being given to the social goal of equality of opportunity —and especially to equality of educational opportunity—added resources will undoubtedly be required to help achieve it.

The format of this study is as follows: Chapter I attempts to lay out the broad conceptual framework within which the various types of benefits and costs can be viewed and to indicate their relevance to legislative policy. It draws the important distinction between equity and economic efficiency and classifies forms of benefits and costs. Chapter II focuses on the benefits of higher education, particularly emphasizing those which are most amenable to measurement; the bulk of attention is devoted to the monetary returns to students via better paying jobs and the monetary returns to the state via increased tax revenues. Chapter III attempts to classify the various types of costs of higher education and indicates by whom these costs are paid. Chapter IV presents information on the extent to which all socioeconomic groups have access to higher education, receive subsidies through their attendance, and repay the subsidy through state and local taxes. In Chapters II–IV the empirical focus is on the state of California.

Chapter V indicates the types of research that still need to be done to enhance our knowledge of the benefits and costs of higher education. Chapter VI provides a short summary of the major policy related findings of the study. Finally, the Epilogue is addressed to issues in the financing of higher education and is only loosely connected with the earlier chapters.

Chapter I

CONCEPTUAL FRAMEWORK
FOR MAKING CHOICES

Planning for higher education—whether in California or elsewhere—requires attention to an enormous number and variety of
issues. These issues can be usefully grouped into three broad
classes: choices among *output* alternatives; choices among *input*
alternatives; choices among *finance* alternatives.

ISSUES AND CHOICES

OUTPUT ISSUES. How much higher education should be provided? What kinds and quality are most appropriate? And how
should eligibility for higher education be determined?
  A. What percentages of all college age males and females
     should the public higher education system attempt to serve?
     Are existing selection criteria adequate? Are they fair?
  B. What should be the relative emphasis on vocational train-
     ing and academic training? Should various kinds of on-
     the-job training be considered as a form of higher educa-
     tion?
  C. What is the optimal mix between graduate and undergrad-
     uate programs?

7

D. Is the average quality of educational output increased or decreased by segmenting the higher education system (for example, into junior colleges, state colleges, and the state university)? How can quality of output be assessed? Is there a failure to distinguish between the quality of *students* and the quality of *education* provided to students?

INPUT ISSUES. In what ways should higher education be provided?

A. What is the most effective mix of education inputs? Are large lectures less effective than small lectures? Always? Sometimes? How effective is independent study? Is there now an appropriate degree of utilization of teaching assistants vis-à-vis regular faculty? Is the presence of a research program necessary to an effective teaching program? Is it helpful?

B. Is it wiser to construct campuses within commuting distance of large population concentrations rather than in more remote areas? Are large campuses more efficient than small ones? How will access by various groups of young people be affected by decisions on the locations of campuses?

FINANCE ISSUES. How should the costs of public higher education be shared?

A. What criteria can be used to decide who should pay what fraction of the costs? What should be the relationship between the financial benefits received from higher education and the payments made in support of it? How much should students and their parents be expected to pay? Should the relationship be made to depend on parents' ability to pay? On the students' post-college income? How much should be paid by the federal government? State government? Local government? Others? From what sources can additional funds be most easily obtained?

B. How can the financial and other barriers preventing the enrollment of qualified people be overcome? Can these barriers be removed most effectively through increased grants, decreased student charges, or additional loan funds? For students from very low income families, are substantial grants—perhaps even in excess of total out-of-pocket costs

—essential for achieving true equality of educational opportunity?

C. Is it efficient and equitable to provide sizable public subsidies to those receiving higher education, while giving nothing to those who are either uninterested or unqualified? Should financial support be provided for people preferring education or vocational training outside a state's public higher education system? Are there grounds for making investment opportunity grants to young people who aspire to become small, independent businessmen, for example, rather than to attend college?

POLICY CHOICES. Such issues as these involve legislative policy choices at a number of different expenditure-control levels:

A. There are decisions involving the aggregate effects of higher education for a state, decisions having to do with the amount of money that should be allocated to the entire higher education process in the state.

B. There are decisions regarding how funds which are to be devoted to higher education should be allocated among the various systems, i.e., junior college, state college, and university systems (assuming the systems are to be retained).

C. Within each system there are decisions regarding the allocation of funds among campuses.

D. There are decisions to be made regarding the allocation of funds among departments or other divisions and activities within campuses.

E. Finally, decisions have to be made regarding internal management control.

The variety of choices to be made with respect to higher education is bewildering. We shall deal, however, with only the first two levels of policy choices, although we will touch upon all three classes of issues—output, input, and finance.

BENEFITS AND COSTS

To provide answers to the variety of questions just enumerated, we need to find answers to a whole set of intermediate questions.

But to even pose these intermediate questions we require some overall framework of analysis. The general framework we employ recognizes that there are inevitably both benefits and costs—that is, advantages and disadvantages—to any course of action. Thus, we pose the intermediate questions in three categories: those having to do with the *benefits* from higher education; those having to do with the *costs* of higher education; and those having to do with *balance between* benefits and costs.

BENEFITS OF HIGHER EDUCATION.

  A. What are the *forms* of benefits? What are their *magnitudes?*
  B. *Which groups* of people receive the benefits? How much is received by the student? How much is received by his employer? How much is returned to the state through increased taxes?
  C. Over what *time periods* are the benefits received?
  D. Do the benefits vary by the *type* of higher education that is provided?

COSTS OF HIGHER EDUCATION.

  A. What are the *forms* or types of costs? What are their magnitudes?
  B. How are the costs *shared:* between students and parents, and taxpayers? Income classes of taxpayers? Taxpayers at various governmental levels (local, state, federal)?

BALANCE BETWEEN BENEFITS AND COSTS.

  A. Are the groups that receive benefits of higher education the same as those that bear the costs?
  B. Are there substantial numbers of persons who receive benefits but do not bear costs?
  C. Are there others who share the costs but receive little, if any, of the benefits?

We cannot provide full answers to these questions, not only because the available data are as yet inadequate, but also because there remain some important conceptual problems to be resolved. We do, however, provide at least partial answers to many of them, and we try to indicate how others might be answered as additional data become available. In Chapters II–IV we develop methods for estimating the magnitudes of benefits and costs, identifying the principal beneficiaries and bearers of costs, and comparing the results of the findings about benefits with those about costs.

Before proceeding, we must understand the forms taken by the benefits and costs. It is no simple matter, however, to decide precisely what a benefit is or what a cost is. And not all forms of benefits or costs may be regarded by all persons as of equal importance. Therefore, the rest of this chapter will set the stage for subsequent ones, by pointing out the general types of effects of higher education (benefits or costs) that deserve attention, even though we shall not be able to deal quantitatively with all of them.

MAJOR CONCEPTUAL DISTINCTIONS

EFFICIENCY EFFECTS vs. EQUITY EFFECTS. The economic efficiency of an activity—here, higher education—involves the degree of success of the activity in producing outputs (trained students) that are more valuable than the resources used up in the process of producing them. The value of output is generally measured by what people are willing to pay for it; and, so, as a first (and minimal) approximation, the value of college education may be measured by the increased salaries that employers are willing to pay for workers who are college educated rather than only high school educated.[1] Efficiency, in the present context, can thus be thought of in terms of the amount by which National Income (or Gross National Product) is raised by higher education.

But, which people receive this increased income? And which pay the costs of the resources—teachers, classrooms, laboratories, etc.—that are required to produce the increased income? In other words, how fairly are the additional incomes and the costs of public education shared? This is the issue of equity.

The distinction between efficiency and equity is essential if we are to come to grips intelligently with difficult issues of public policy.[2] To illustrate: it may be accepted that higher education is

---

[1] But this is *only* a first approximation of the full value of college education, because it disregards benefits that arise in ways other than through the job market. We return to this point below, in Chapter II.

[2] For a discussion and application of these concepts, though in a quite different context, see W. Lee Hansen and Burton A. Weisbrod, "The Economics of the Military Draft," *Quarterly Journal of Economics,* LXXXI (August, 1967), 395–421.

efficient in raising incomes, but it might be objected, nevertheless, that the method of financing higher education is inequitable. By contrast, it might be felt by some that higher education is being financed equitably, but that it is really not an efficient way to utilize resources—that there are better ways to increase people's real incomes (such as by devoting more resources to improving technology). Of course, there are intermediate positions in which various degrees of inefficiency and inequity are adjudged to exist.

The point is that disagreements on matters of policy are more likely to be resolved if each participant recognizes when, and to what extent, the dispute centers on factual matters of efficiency and when it centers on value judgments regarding the fairness of the distribution of benefits and costs. This is not to deny, however, that both classes of issues are difficult to resolve, for the factual data relevant to assessment of efficiency are scarce, as is consensus on what should be regarded as equitable.

It may be useful to note an important way in which social objectives of efficiency and equity can sometimes conflict. Considerations of efficiency might suggest that higher education should not be provided to all youngsters—after all, society might well assume (and in fact it does) that not every youth can benefit from higher education by an amount commensurate with the cost of the schooling. But such a policy inevitably produces questions of equity.

Is it fair for some young people to receive public subsidies while others do not? If every young person were not only offered the opportunity to go to college for four years, but were required to go, then all youth would receive a similar public subsidy. But if this is more equitable it is doubtless less efficient, for all youth are not likely to benefit enough to cover the costs of resources required to educate them. Accordingly, the conflict between equity and economic efficiency in higher education planning appears to be a genuine one.

INVESTMENT EFFECTS VS. CONSUMPTION EFFECTS. The tendency to assess the economic efficiency of higher education by reference to its effect on income-earning capacity involves an oversimplification. Higher education does more than merely raise incomes. References to the income-generating effects of higher education imply a view of education as an investment from which monetary returns are expected to flow, just as such returns are expected from investment in business factories and equipment. Indeed, these types of investments do have common attributes.[3] But they also have differences. Higher education is an investment, but it is more.

It is also a consumer good—something which people buy because they like it, not just because it will help to raise their incomes. This is the reason that we said above that measuring the value of college education by the increased salaries college graduates can earn is only a first approximation. Consumption benefits from higher education, including such benefits as the possibly increased enjoyment of life, are particularly difficult to measure, but their relevance should not be dismissed.

PRIVATE EFFECTS vs. SOCIAL EFFECTS. Both investment and consumption benefits have been discussed from the point of view of those receiving the education. While such benefits may be realized by students and their families—internal effects—other persons may also be affected—external effects. In more general usage external effects are frequently termed social, while the internal effects are termed private.

Recognition of the possible existence of external or social effects from higher education is exceedingly important because of what it might imply for the issue of what proportion of the cost of higher education should be borne by students and their parents, and what proportion should be borne by the public—that is, by taxpayers in general, either in the state or nationally. It might be argued that all, or at least a very large fraction of the costs of higher education, should be borne by the student and his family *if* the returns in the form of increased income to the student are large. However, this important policy conclusion could be overturned if the social (or external) benefits of higher education were also large—that is, if benefits of higher education to persons other than the students and their families were substantial. The economic theory of external effects is well established, but assessment of empirical magnitudes of such effects is extremely difficult. However, some attention will be given to the feasibility of estimating orders of magnitude for external effects.

BENEFITS TO A STATE vs. BENEFITS TO INDIVIDUALS. Recognition of the distinction between private benefits (to students and their families) and social benefits (to others) leads to the distinction be-

[3] See, for example, *Journal of Political Economy, Supplement* (October, 1962).

tween those benefits from higher education which are realized within the state that offers the education and those which are realized outside of it. This distinction is important because of the degree to which college trained people are likely to migrate from the state.

It is generally true that a college trained individual does not suffer in terms of income if he leaves the state in which he was educated for a well paying job elsewhere. Thus, the benefits to the individual from his higher education tend to be realized by the individual wherever he may be located.

At the same time, the tax system may be viewed, in part, as a means by which some of the public investment in higher education is recompensed. If an individual's earnings are increased by virtue of the publicly provided college education he receives, then the increase in his income will lead to an increase in his income tax, sales tax, and other tax liabilities; and these increases may be regarded as a return to taxpayers in general on the investment which they made in his education.

It follows that the out-migration of a person who was publicly educated involves a geographical relocation of the increase in the tax base represented by that person's increased income—a relocation that moves the tax base from the political jurisdiction supplying the higher education to some other jurisdiction. Out-migration of a publicly educated person mitigates against taxpayers in the state obtaining a return on their investments,[4] though it also diminishes need for public services.

At the same time that an area is experiencing out-migration, it is, of course, also receiving in-migration of persons educated elsewhere. Much of the in-migration, however, presumably occurs independently of the area's (state's) extensive system of public higher education. This is a significant point which will be discussed further in Chapter II.

EXPLICIT MONEY COSTS VS. IMPLICIT COSTS.   If we are interested in people's responses to changes in costs of higher education, we must realize that a cost should be interpreted as something which is given up. When someone attends a college, he (or his family)

---

[4] For further discussion, see Burton A. Weisbrod, *External Benefits of Public Education* (Princeton, N.J.: Industrial Relations Section, Princeton University, 1964). Also, Harry Johnson, "The Economics of the 'Brain Drain': The Canadian Case," *Minerva* (Spring, 1965), pp. 299–312.

normally gives up some money for fees or tuition, for books, and —if he lives away from home—for room and board.

But the student gives up more than what is reflected by his cash payments. He also gives up time which he might otherwise use to work and produce income; in short, he foregoes income. Thus, it is important to recognize that costs of higher education are not limited to explicit payments. The true cost of higher education would not be zero, even if the student were to live at home, require no books and supplies, and pay absolutely no fees or tuition! We shall, in Chapter III, discuss this matter further and provide some quantitative estimates.

INSTITUTIONAL COSTS vs. NON–INSTITUTIONAL COSTS. All costs —whether in money or non-money form—must be met somehow. How these costs are shared by students, their parents, and various classes of taxpayers—through the state budget—involves important equity issues. But it is also in part a matter of efficiency, in the sense that the pricing system—tuition, fees, student charges, etc.— can be expected to influence the amount of higher education that is demanded, and thereby, to affect the total money cost of a higher education system. Thus, it is important to note that the method of financing and the total amount to be financed are intertwined.

This discussion of types of benefits and costs, and of their forms and magnitudes, serves as the backdrop for the analytic and quantitative work in the remainder of this study. It also serves as an aid to the consideration of policy issues, for we can now view the various issues in terms of this framework of benefit and cost concepts.

We end this chapter with an illustration. Consider the question: Should a state that has an extensive system of public junior colleges (JC's) expand the system? Contract it? While we do not answer these questions, it should be helpful to point out that the answers rest partially on whether the JC's are *efficient*—that is, whether they produce benefits in excess of costs—bearing in mind that costs include foregone earnings as well as explicit payments, while benefits include both those received by students and those received by others (external benefits).

More than efficiency is relevant, though. There are important *equity* considerations. Should access to a four-year public college be restricted to those who will benefit substantially from it, with others diverted to junior colleges or excluded from higher education altogether? If the answer is "yes," i.e., some young people are judged to be ineligible for higher education or eligible only for the relatively low cost JC education, should those who are excluded receive a compensatory subsidy so as not to be penalized?

And on the finance side, how much of the cost of JC's should be borne by students? By their parents? By local taxpayers? By state taxpayers? By federal taxpayers? What criteria should be used for deciding how the cost burden should be shared—in the interests of achieving equity and efficiency?

It is with the faith—to some degree born out of experience—that clarification of issues and presentation of relevant data will be helpful for problem solving that we proceed.

Chapter II

BENEFITS OF PUBLIC HIGHER EDUCATION IN CALIFORNIA

Higher education is believed to produce a wide variety of benefits both for students and for others.[1] Some of these are in monetary form, others are non-monetary in nature. Some are easily quantifiable while others are not. The bulk of this chapter is devoted to presenting estimates in monetary terms of some of the important benefits of higher education as they apply to the state of California. Later in this chapter we shall discuss some of the important non-monetary benefits. We begin with a review of several important concepts which are relevant to what follows.

FORMS OF BENEFITS

In Chapter I we identified a class of investment returns from higher education. These returns result from the apparent increase in labor productivity that higher education brings. Evidence of the

---

[1] For further discussion see Burton A. Weisbrod, "Education and Investment in Human Capital," *Journal of Political Economy, Supplement* (October, 1962).

increased productivity is the significant differential in earnings of college graduates, and even of persons having a partial college education (non-graduates), as compared with high school graduates of the same age, sex, and color. Table II-1 shows, for Californians, the consistent pattern of incomes increasing with level of education.[2] A similar pattern, presented in Table II-2 where the data are also broken down by age and color, is found for the United States as a whole.

TABLE II-1. MEDIAN INCOMES BY LEVEL OF SCHOOLING, SEX, AND COLOR, FOR PERSONS IN CALIFORNIA AGE 25 AND OVER, 1959

	High School Graduates	Persons With Some College Education	4 or More Years of College
Sex and Color			
Total			
Males	$6,039	$6,399	$8,108
Females	2,557	2,800	4,151
Non-White			
Males	4,372	4,698	5,820
Females	2,173	2,709	3,860

Source: U.S. Bureau of the Census, U.S. Census of Population, 1960, *Detailed Characteristics, California*, Final Report PC(1)–6D (U.S. Government Printing Office, Washington, D.C.), Table 138, p. 6–945.

Data such as those shown in Tables II-1 and II-2 give a somewhat exaggerated picture of the extent to which higher education raises productivity and income. There is strong reason to believe that those persons who go on to college, and especially those who graduate, are in general more able and ambitious than are those who do not enter college. Thus, college-going students would subsequently be expected to earn more than non-college-going students even if they did not continue their education. Recent work suggests that approximately 25 percent of the observed differential in earnings between college and high school graduates is attributable not

[2] Ideally, we want to view earnings rather than income as reflecting the payoff to education, since income includes money returns from the ownership of other forms of capital.

TABLE II-2. MEDIAN INCOMES BY LEVEL OF SCHOOLING, SEX, AND COLOR, FOR SELECTED AGE GROUPS, U.S., 1959

Sex, Color, and Age		High School Graduates	Persons With Some College Education	College Graduates 4 Years of College	College Graduates 5 Years or More of College
All					
Males	30–34	$5,452	$6,055	$7,365	$7,250
	35–44	5,848	6,772	8,669	9,091
	45–54	5,806	6,772	8,949	9,827
Females	30–34	2,183	2,287	2,768	4,036
	35–44	2,360	2,638	3,231	4,620
	45–54	2,612	3,011	4,021	5,365
Non-White					
Males	30–34	3,779	4,209	4,732	5,167
	35–44	4,193	4,554	5,051	5,998
	45–54	3,939	4,301	4,778	6,215
Females	30–34	1,819	2,316	3,406	4,246
	35–44	1,974	2,547	3,656	4,670
	45–54	1,784	2,360	3,706	4,832

Source: U.S. Bureau of the Census, U.S. Census of Population, 1960, Subject Reports, *Educational Attainment*, Final Report PC(2)–5B (U.S. Government Printing Office, Washington, D.C.), Tables 6, 7, pp. 88, 89, 112, 113, and 114.

to schooling at all, but to these other factors of ability and motivation.[3]

Even after a downward adjustment for differences in ability, about three-fourths of the difference in income remains as a financial return or payoff from higher education. Moreover, this payoff does not arise in a single year or even in several years; it continues, on average, throughout one's working lifetime, as the data in Table II-2 suggest. Recognition of this continuing return from higher education has led to the popular statement that a college

[3] Burton A. Weisbrod and Peter Karpoff, "Monetary Returns to College Education," *Review of Economics and Statistics* (November, 1968), pp. 491–97. Gary S. Becker, *Human Capital* (N.Y.: Princeton University Press, 1964), p. 82, estimated that only 12 percent of the differential is attributable to such non-schooling factors. Edward F. Denison estimated that 40 percent of the differential is attributable to ability, in *The Sources of Economic Growth* (Committee for Economic Development, Washington, D.C., 1962), p. 69.

education is worth $100,000 or more over one's lifetime. Such a statement, based on a simple adding up of anticipated larger incomes for college-educated persons, not only errs because of the ability factor; it also errs because it disregards the fact that, for a student at age eighteen or twenty, extra income expected ten, twenty, or forty years from now is certainly not equivalent to income today and therefore cannot be simply added to extra income expected immediately.

To account for this fact that income in the present is worth more than income in the future—if for no other reason than that present income can be invested at interest—we employ the present value concept which assigns lesser importance to income the further into the future it is expected. The present value of the extra lifetime income that a college trained person can expect is substantially smaller than what one would get simply by adding up all of the annual sums of additional income expected. We will shortly estimate the present value of the additional incomes that college trained persons can expect.[4]

Another important point is that all of the increases in income that college students can expect will not be retained by them. The tax system—at the federal, state, and local levels—acts to transfer to taxpayers in general a portion of all increases in income. Only the remainder constitutes an internal or private benefit to the student.

The magnitude of private benefits may not be affected by changes in a person's location, but the particular governmental unit receiving the taxes is, of course, greatly dependent on whether migration occurs. Thus, when it is recognized that many of the persons educated in the California higher education system will leave the state in subsequent years, the result is that the state of California will lose some tax revenue that it would otherwise receive. At the same time, though, the demands on the state treasury to provide public services will also diminish through the out-

[4] An alternative approach is to think of educational expenditures as an investment yielding an internal rate of return, analogous to the rate of return earned on other types of investments; see W. L. Hansen, "Total and Private Rates of Return to Investment in Schooling," *Journal of Political Economy,* LXXI (April, 1963), 128–40. However, we do not follow this approach since we want to focus more explicitly on benefits and costs.

migration process.[5] The fiscal loss to the state, therefore, is only the difference, if any, between the loss in tax revenue and the saving in public service costs.

It is, of course, true that at the same time some persons are out-migrating, others are in-migrating and thereby producing off-setting effects, e.g., more tax revenues. However, it is not clear that the in-migration and the accompanying tax revenues are a consequence of the California higher education system. Insofar as the in-migration would occur anyway, its effects are not relevant to an assessment of the effects of the higher education system.

These, then, are the types of considerations relevant to evaluating the monetary effects of the California higher education system —its effects on students, and through the tax system, its effects on others.

EMPIRICAL ESTIMATES

Employing the concepts discussed above, we now present and describe the bases for our estimates of some of the private and social financial returns from public higher education in California. Before doing so, however, we note that the returns are not, in general, peculiar to *public* higher education. The implication of this fact is that if students were to attend private colleges instead of public ones, we would expect essentially the same total private and public returns. But some young people would not be able to obtain higher education were it not for the relatively lower cost of public institutions. Hence, the fact that a system of higher education is public produces a differently constituted student body.

The bulk of the California system of higher education—and the bulk of the state's support for higher education—is addressed to undergraduate education. We concentrate attention, therefore, on undergraduate education, although we will discuss graduate education later.

UNDERGRADUATE EDUCATION OF MALES. The magnitude of financial benefits for male college graduates and also for other

[5] Mortality, in this context, is similar to out-migration insofar as the state treasury is concerned, although from the standpoint of the nation as a whole the two are, of course, quite different in their impacts.

people, through the state and local, and the federal tax systems, is shown in Table II-3. Line 1, column 1, indicates that as of the year 1965 male college graduates were receiving greater incomes than high school graduates.[6] The amounts were such that if a college

TABLE II-3. ESTIMATED FINANCIAL RETURNS FROM HIGHER EDUCATION TO AN AVERAGE CALIFORNIA MALE COLLEGE GRADUATE, TO THE CALIFORNIA STATE AND LOCAL TREASURIES, AND TO THE U.S. TREASURY, 1965

| | *Lifetime Additional Income per College Graduate* | *Lifetime Additional Taxes Paid per College Graduate to* | |
		California State and Local Governments	*Federal Government*
Category of Return			
1. Total, unadjusted	$118,000	$11,800	$21,200
2. Less: Adjustment for ability differences	29,000	2,900	5,300
3. Sub-Total	$ 89,000	$ 8,900	$15,900
4. Less: Adjustment for out-migration and mortality	—	4,700	—
5. Total, net	$ 89,000	$ 4,200	$15,900
6. Net adjusted for time pattern (present value*)	$ 20,900	$ 1,000	$ 3,800

Sources: Based upon our estimates of incomes and taxes from data in: (a) U.S. Bureau of Census, U.S. Census of Population, 1960, Subject Reports: *Line 1—Educational Attainment; Line 4—Lifetime and Recent Migration.* (b) Levern F. Graves, "State and Local Tax Burdens in California: The Property Tax Compared with State Taxes," *Taxation of Property in California,* Part 5 (California State Legislature, December, 1964), Table XXX, p. 45. (c) Internal Revenue Service, *Instructions for Preparing Your Federal Income Tax Return, Form 1040.*

* Present values computed at 5 percent discount rate.

graduate in 1965 were to have the same income experience over his working lifetime as indicated by the average (median) data for 1965, he would receive $118,000 additional income.[7]

Such estimates disregard the possibility that income differences

[6] Those readers interested in learning more about the exact methods of computation which were followed are referred to the Appendix to this chapter.

[7] Lifetime additional gross income of $118,000 per male college graduate was arrived at by taking, first, 1959 median earnings of males in the United

may grow through time, not simply because of inflation but because of technological and other changes that may enhance the market value of college graduates relative to high school graduates. Although this has happened in recent years,[8] it may or may not continue as an increasing percentage of young people complete college and thereby tend to depress income differentials for college graduates. Changes in labor demand patterns could, however, offset this tendency, as has occurred during the post-World War II period.

Our estimate in Table II-3, of $118,000 total unadjusted return, is an overstatement because it is derived from data on incomes of persons with four years *or more* of college education. Unfortunately, this is the only form in which the data for California are currently available. That the resulting overstatement of returns to a college graduate (four years only) is relatively small, however, is suggested by a comparison of data on median earnings of all United States persons age twenty-five or over having, respectively, four years of college education, and five or more years, as shown in Table II-4. For 1965, the latter group—which contained two-thirds as many persons—had a median income of $9,613, only 10 percent higher than the median income of $8,748 for the larger group of those completing four years of college.[9]

To continue with the description of Table II-3, columns 2 and 3 show the extent to which part of the additional income obtained by college graduates is returned to various levels of gov-

---

States by age and education from the 1960 Census (1960 Census of Population, Volume PC(2)-5B, *Educational Attainment*, Table 6), and then multiplying by the approximate average labor force participation rate, about 94 percent for adult males. These medians were adjusted to conform to California incomes in 1965 by upward proportional adjustments ranging from 1.14 to 1.37 depending upon educational level. This yields a set of incomes by age and education which we estimate to represent the 1965 distribution of California mean incomes, for males, by age and education.

The income differences by education at each age group were summed (each appropriately weighted for the number of years to which it applied) to yield the additional lifetime income. A similar procedure was used to estimate the income of California females.

[8] See Herman P. Miller, "Lifetime Income and Economic Growth," *American Economic Review*, LV (September, 1965), 834–44.

[9] U.S. Bureau of the Census, "Income in 1965 of Families and Persons in the United States," *Current Population Reports* (Series P-60, No. 51, U.S. Government Printing Office, Washington, D.C., 1967), p. 34.

ernment through the tax system. For the combined state and local governments in California we estimate the tax rate on additional

TABLE II-4. MEDIAN INCOMES BY LEVEL OF SCHOOLING, SEX, AND COLOR, FOR PERSONS AGE 25 AND OVER, U.S., 1965

	High School Graduates	Total	Persons With Some College	Persons With 4 Years of College	Persons With 5 or More Years of College
Sex and Color					
Males, Total	$6,458	$8,076	$7,222	$8,748	$9,613
White	6,575	8,408	N.A.	N.A.	N.A.
Non-White	4,544	5,589	N.A.	N.A.	N.A.
Females, Total	2,544	3,553	2,676	4,293	5,670
White	2,576	3,516	N.A.	N.A.	N.A.
Non-White	2,271	4,047	N.A.	N.A.	N.A.

Source: U.S. Bureau of the Census, "Income in 1965 of Families and Persons in the United States," *Current Population Reports* (Series P-60, No. 51, U.S. Government Printing Office, Washington, D.C., 1967), Table 21, p. 34.

N.A.: Data not available.

income to be about 10 percent,[10] and for the federal government, 18 percent.[11] Thus, in column 2, line 1 (Table II-3), the figure

[10] This is based on L. F. Graves' estimate that state and local taxes in California comprise about 12 percent of income *after* federal taxes at the $7,500–$9,999 level. Federal income tax averages about 10 percent of income at this level; thus, to find the average state and local tax rate on income *before* federal tax we must reduce the 12 percent Graves' estimate by 10 percent of itself, to 10.8 percent. For simplicity and to avoid the implication of greater precision than is justified, we have rounded this down to 10 percent, as the average state and local tax rate applicable to gross income. Over much of the income range the California tax system as a whole is approximately proportional at this 10 percent level; this is to say that about 10 percent of each additional dollar of income goes into taxes. (See Levern F. Graves, "State and Local Tax Burdens in California: The Property Tax Compared with State Taxes," *Taxation of Property in California*, Part 5 [California Legislature, December, 1964], Table XXX, p. 45.)

[11] We have assumed that everyone uses the standard 10 percent deduction and that a 20 percent marginal rate is applicable to everyone in the system. The first assumption overstates the additional tax yield, and the second understates it. On balance we believe the overstatement is smaller than the understatement, since many people confront marginal rates of more than 20 percent. We believe our estimates of the federal tax benefit are on the whole conservative—that is, likely to be an understatement.

is 10 percent of the $118,000 income figure in column 1, and the figure in column 3 is 18 percent of $118,000.

So far, we have shown in Table II-3 the difference in lifetime income associated with the difference in educational attainment of college graduates and high school graduates. We have shown, further, how much of that difference is, on average, shared by the income recipient with government.

As we pointed out in Chapter I, it would be erroneous to ascribe all the observed differences in income to education. There is strong reason to believe that persons with higher levels of educational attainment have, on the whole, greater ability and motivation. Consequently, they would be expected to earn more than their less educated counterparts, even if they did not have more education. As noted above, recent research leads us to believe that approximately 25 percent of the differentials indicated are attributable to these factors; as a result, we judge that the lifetime financial return to a four year college education in California is about 25 percent less than the $118,000 amount shown in Table II-3. Line 2 of the table reflects the ability factor adjustment, and line 3 shows the adjusted increase in income and in tax receipts.

Line 4 is included in recognition of the fact that some of the $8,900 of increased taxes that the state of California or its subdivisions might expect will not be received because college graduates will out-migrate or, though far less commonly, will die prior to the end of the normal working lifetime. Based on data for California from the 1960 Census of Population, Table II-5 shows the percentage, of male Californians, age twenty, that may be expected to remain in the state at various subsequent ages. It is startling to note that by age thirty, only 66 percent remain, a full one-third having already left—nearly all by migration rather than by death.[12] From a narrow fiscal viewpoint, adjustment for this factor leads to a further reduction in taxes paid of $4,700 shown in Table II-3, line 4, column 2. The state and local governments receive, as a result, an average of only $4,200 in taxes per male college graduate (line 5), not the $8,900 they would receive in the absence of out-migration or mortality during the working years.

[12] The only available data are for all males, regardless of educational level. Migration among college educated males is probably even greater than what is shown in Table II-5.

Neither the total return to the individual (column 1) nor to the federal government (column 3) is affected by the out-migration adjustment; we assume that one's income is, in general, not substantially affected by migration, although if it is, income is likely to be increased. Thus, the principal financial effect of out-migration

TABLE II-5. PERCENTAGE OF CALIFORNIA MALES, AGE 20, OUT-MIGRATING, DYING, AND REMAINING IN CALIFORNIA, BY VARIOUS SUBSEQUENT AGES

	Percentage Out-Migrating	Percentage Dying in California	Percentage Remaining in California
Age			
20	—	—	100.0%
25	22.2%	0.7%	77.1
30	10.2	0.5	66.4
35	6.0	0.5	59.8
40	4.7	0.7	54.4
45	3.0	1.1	50.3
50	2.4	1.6	46.2
55	1.8	2.5	42.0
60	1.1	3.7	37.2

Sources: U.S. Bureau of the Census, Census of Population, 1960, Subject Reports, *Recent and Lifetime Migration*, PC(2)-2D, Table 8, pp. 430–93; and U.S. Vital Statistics in *Statistical Abstract of the United States, 1966*, p. 68. Percent out-migrating based on 1955–60 experience of 1955 Pacific Region residents born in that region; Californians comprise about 75 percent of the residents of the Pacific Region, but no separate data are available for California.

in the present context is on the *particular* state and local government that receives the taxes (and provides the public services).

It is clear that college education does not increase income only temporarily, but over the entire working lifetime. If one looks at these increases—or the derivative tax-revenue increases—from the time perspective of a student-age person, it is apparent that while some portions of the added income (and taxes) are expected to be realized quite promptly, other portions are expected ten, twenty, thirty or forty or more years later. As we stated earlier in this chapter, neither students nor state and local tax authorities are indifferent between revenue now and revenue in the future. In Table II-3, line 6 therefore shows that the present value of the additional lifetime income attributable to college education is $20,900, compared with the $89,000 value obtained without con-

sidering the time pattern of income.[13] Viewed in this light—the
light in which, incidentally, an ordinary investment is viewed in
business capital markets—higher education is a good deal less
valuable than is commonly believed.

Table II-3 also shows that the values of additional tax payments are reduced, similarly, when the present value weightings
are made—to $1,000 of present value of additional state and local
taxes, and to $3,800 of additional federal taxes.

TABLE II-6. ESTIMATED FINANCIAL RETURNS FROM HIGHER
EDUCATION TO AN AVERAGE CALIFORNIA NON-GRADUATING
MALE, TO CALIFORNIA STATE AND LOCAL TREASURIES,
AND TO THE U.S. TREASURY, 1965

	Lifetime Additional Income per Non-Graduate	Lifetime Additional Taxes Paid to	
		California State and Local Governments	Federal Government
Category of Return			
1. Total, unadjusted	$27,200	$2,700	$4,900
2. Less: Adjustment for ability differences	6,800	700	1,200
3. Sub-Total	$20,400	$2,000	$3,700
4. Less: Adjustment for out-migration and mortality	—	1,000	—
5. Total, net	$20,400	$1,000	$3,700
6. Net, adjusted for time pattern (present value*)	$ 3,900	$ 200	$ 700

Source: Same as for Table II-3.
* Present values computed at 5 percent discount rate.

Now that we have reviewed the format and meaning of Table
II-3, we can present, with far less discussion, a set of similar tables

[13] The precise formula for the Present Value (V) is:

$$V = \sum_{t=0}^{N} \frac{B_t}{(1 + r)^t}, \text{ where } B_t \text{ equals benefits in year } t,$$

r is the discount (interest) rate, and t is the number of years elapsed since
completion of school, and N is the time horizon. There continues to be
disagreement on precisely what discount rate is the "appropriate" one to

TABLE II-7. ESTIMATED FINANCIAL RETURNS FROM HIGHER
EDUCATION TO AN AVERAGE CALIFORNIA FEMALE COLLEGE
GRADUATE, TO THE CALIFORNIA STATE AND LOCAL
TREASURIES, AND TO THE U.S. TREASURY, 1965

	Lifetime Additional Income per College Graduate	Lifetime Additional Taxes Paid to	
		California State and Local Governments	Federal Government
Category of Return			
1. Total, unadjusted	$55,700	$5,600	$10,000
2. Less: Adjustment for ability differences	13,900	1,400	2,500
3. Sub-Total	$41,800	$4,200	$ 7,500
4. Less: Adjustment for out-migration and mortality	—	2,000	—
5. Total, net	$41,800	$2,200	$ 7,500
6. Net, adjusted for time pattern (present value*)	$11,000	$ 700	$ 2,000

Source: Same as for Table II-3, except *Educational Attainment*, Table 7, rather than Table 6.

* Present values computed at 5 percent discount rate.

for a number of different groups of students. Table II-6 shows the financial returns for males who obtain some college education in California, but who do not graduate.[14] This table shows that the unadjusted lifetime return for non-graduates is about $27,000, compared with the $118,000 for college graduates (Table II-3). The adjusted return, in present value terms, is $3,900; of this amount

use in calculating present values. Some advocate using discount rates as low as 2 or 3 percent, while others argue for 10 percent or more. We opt for a middle position and use a 5 percent rate. This is consistent with the Joint Economic Committee's recent recommendation that "the current minimum-risk interest rate which should be used for evaluating public investments is at least 5 percent." Professional debate continues, however, on the appropriate meaning of risk in connection with discounting (see Joint Economic Committee, U.S. Congress, *Economic Analysis of Public Investment Decisions: Interest Rate Policy and Discounting Analysis* [Washington, D.C.: U.S. Government Printing Office, 1968], p. 16). We would have preferred to use several different discount rates so as to test the sensitivity of the results; however, we decided not to do this because of the difficulties of exposition.

[14] We assume that persons receiving some college education average two years of schooling.

$200 is in the form of state and local taxes and $700 in federal taxes.

UNDERGRADUATE EDUCATION OF FEMALES. Table II-7 presents our estimates for female college graduates in California. Compared with the estimates in Table II-3, for males, we see that from a financial investment point of view, the return for women college graduates is markedly smaller than that for men, $56,000 versus $118,000, as is the return to state and local governments, $700 versus $1,000, in present value terms.

Table II-8 presents our estimates of monetary returns for females who obtained some college education. The returns are, as expected, smaller than for female graduates and also decidedly smaller than for male non-graduates.

TABLE II-8. ESTIMATED FINANCIAL RETURNS FROM HIGHER EDUCATION TO AN AVERAGE CALIFORNIA NON-GRADUATING FEMALE, TO THE CALIFORNIA STATE AND LOCAL TREASURIES, AND TO THE U.S. TREASURY, 1965

	Lifetime Additional Income per Non-Graduate	Lifetime Additional Taxes Paid to	
		California State and Local Governments	Federal Government
Category of Return			
1. Total, unadjusted	$14,900	$1,500	$2,700
2. Less: Adjustment for ability differences	3,700	400	700
3. Sub-Total	$11,200	$1,100	$2,000
4. Less: Adjustment for out-migration and mortality	—	400	—
5. Total, net	$11,200	$ 700	$2,000
6. Net, adjusted for time pattern (present value*)	$ 3,200	$ 200	$ 600

Source: Same as for Table II-7.
* Present values computed at 5 percent discount rate.

Much of the difference in monetary returns for males and females results because the percentage of females having jobs that produce money income is smaller than it is for males (that is, the labor force participation rate is lower for females); and women who work are more likely than men to work only part-time. Were it not for these factors the differences would be much smaller. Although the data are not shown in the accompanying tables, the financial value of college education for that subset of women college graduates who work *regularly* over the years until age 65 is $17,000 in present value terms, compared to $22,000 for *regularly-employed* males. This difference of $5,000 in the present values of incomes of *regularly-employed* males and females is only about half the difference of $9,900 ($20,900 minus $11,000) between *all* males and females, as shown in Tables II-3 and II-7.

Although we have shown that females, on the average, gain less financially from college education than males, our analysis has been incomplete. Higher education for women also has an effect on their subsequent ability to educate a family, and since much informal education takes place in the home, this effect of a woman's higher education can be significant.[15] Although this intergenerational effect of higher education is not limited to women, its strength is probably greater than it is for men, who normally spend less time with their children.

There is another aspect of the benefits from higher education for women that we feel justifies further study. Assume that there was no investment return whatsoever from higher education for women—that is, assume that women never held jobs outside the home, nor did their higher education contribute to the raising of their children. College education for women might still be important so long as men were obtaining it. This is to suggest that college educated men prefer to marry college educated women. The importance of this consumer effect of higher education is not known; neither has consideration been given to the degree to which public subsidies are justified in support of it.

SUMMARY OF RESULTS. Our estimates of the monetary value of public higher education per student in California—to males and females, for graduates and non-graduates—can now be summarized in Table II-9. In 1965 approximately 170,000 students—109,000 males and 60,000 females—entered the three California systems of higher education for the first time.[16] On the basis of recent experience it may be expected that of this group about 14 percent of

[15] See William J. Swift and Burton A. Weisbrod, "On the Monetary Value of Education's Intergenerational Effects," *Journal of Political Economy,* LXXIII (December, 1965), 643–49.

[16] The data are based on the number of full-time equivalent students. See *Total and Full-Time Enrollment: California Institutions of Higher Education, Fall 1965* (Sacramento: Department of Finance, March, 1966).

TABLE II-9. PRESENT VALUE* OF BENEFITS FROM PUBLICLY SUPPORTED HIGHER EDUCATION IN CALIFORNIA, 1965

Education Level and Sex	(1) Number Expected	(2) Average Present Value of Added Income per Student	Present Value of Added Income, All Students (1) × (2) (in millions)	Present Value of Added California State and Local Tax Payments (in millions)	Present Value of Added Federal Tax Payments (in millions)
College Graduates					
Males	14,583	$20,900	$305	—	—
Females	8,086	11,000	89	—	—
Total	22,669		$394		
Non-Graduates					
Males	94,856	$ 3,900	$370	—	—
Females	52,283	3,200	167	—	—
Total	147,139		$537		
All (Graduates & Non-Graduates)					
Males	109,439	—	$675	$67	$121
Females	60,369	—	256	26	46
Total	169,808		$931	$93	$167

Sources: Our calculations based on data in *Total and Full-Time Enrollment: California Institutions of Higher Education, Fall 1965* (Sacramento: Department of Finance, March, 1966), pp. 11, 21, 37; in footnotes 9 and 10 above; in Tables II-3, II-7, and II-8; and in Chapter IV, below.

* Present Values computed as of age 18, using a five percent rate of discount.

both males and females will earn baccalaureate degrees[17]—with the balance, of course, being non-graduates. These numbers are entered in column 1. When the expected numbers of graduates and non-graduates, by sex, are multiplied by the respective present values of additional lifetime income, as obtained from Tables II-3, II-6, II-7, and II-8, we obtain a rough estimate of the total capital value—monetary benefits—of the public higher education that will be received by the 1965 cohort of California students (column 3). Finally, columns 4 and 5 indicate the present values of the additional taxes that may be expected by California state and local governments and by the federal government. Of course, substantially larger sums of revenue will in fact be obtained over the following four decades or so—amounts which, when related back to age eighteen when college education normally begins, are translated into the present values we have indicated.

A WORD ON JUNIOR COLLEGES

Our estimates in Table II-9 of the monetary value of public higher education for a given cohort of college age people indicate that the returns are, as expected, larger for those who graduate than for those who do not. It does not follow from this finding that the California Junior Colleges perform a function that is of small value compared to the four year schools.

To begin with, the levels of costs are quite different—a subject to be examined in Chapter III. Beyond this, it should be clear that the Junior Colleges are more than institutions for providing one or two year instructional programs; they also provide, for students who are uncertain as to their academic interests, an opportunity to delay a decision on whether they wish to pursue a four year course of study. Finally, they give many students a second chance to qualify for either the State Colleges or the University of California. In this manner the Junior Colleges provide students with an option to shift to a four year program at a subsequent time, if

[17] This is considerably lower than the national average completion rate of perhaps 50 percent. The relatively low overall rate for California reflects the exceptionally high proportion of California high school graduates who go to junior colleges offering one or two year terminal programs. Unpublished data from the U.S. Office of Education indicate that California ranks 49*th* among the states in the proportion of undergraduates in public institutions who graduate.

they can qualify. This option has a value, as do other kinds of options in the world of commerce.[18]

The approximate number of students who take advantage of the option afforded by the Junior Colleges turns out to be of consequence. In 1965 about 16,000 students transferred from the Junior Colleges to the State Colleges and the University. Almost 3,000 of these transfers were to the University, less than half of them having originally been eligible for University attendance. (No comparable figures on State College eligibility of transferees are available, but we would expect that a substantial fraction did qualify via Junior College attendance.)[19] It is significant that without this option many of the students would probably have been unable to complete a full four year program of higher education.

GRADUATE EDUCATION

Just as undergraduate education provides a monetary payoff, so does graduate education. But estimating the monetary returns from graduate education is a more complex and difficult undertaking—complex because unresolved conceptual issues arise in the consideration of graduate education, and difficult because of the absence of a firm data base.

What are the conceptual issues? Graduate education is not as clear-cut a product or output as is undergraduate education. It is really several products: graduate students are beneficiaries or outputs of education; but, they are also contributors—as teaching assistants —to the undergraduate teaching program; and, they are contributors—as research assistants—to the faculty research process.

The first product—graduate education—involves costs of in-

[18] Research has been done on the valuation of such options in the context of education; see Burton A. Weisbrod, "Education and Investment in Human Capital," *Journal of Political Economy, Supplement* (October, 1962), pp. 106–23.

[19] The data presented in this paragraph are from: CCHE, *Feasibility and Desirability of Eliminating Lower Division Programs at Selected Campuses of the University of California and the California State Colleges* (mimeo), January 6, 1967 (this is a preliminary version of the report), Table 8, p. 69. Also, CCHE, *The Flow of Students Into, Among, and Through the Public Institutions of Higher Education in California, February Report 1967,* (mimeo), May 23, 1967, Table III-3, p. 52.

struction and capital, just as does undergraduate instruction, though such costs are usually several times those required at the undergraduate level. On the benefit side, graduate training, also like undergraduate training, produces men and women who are more productive and who can expect to earn more income as a consequence of their training.

The other two products—teaching and research assistants—also produce financial benefits. These benefits come during the period of graduate education itself, in the form of stipends to graduate students —internal benefits—and in the form of reduced undergraduate teaching costs and reduced costs of faculty research—external benefits. But since these are joint products (they are produced concurrently, as the result of a single integrated production process), the question is how can we disentangle them, if indeed this is possible at all.

Consider undergraduate teaching. This input to teaching could be performed by instructors rather than by graduate teaching assistants (T.A.'s). To the extent that it is done by T.A.'s, the cost of undergraduate education will be lower than would otherwise be the case. If we can assume that the quality of teaching is roughly similar (the evidence to the contrary is not strong!), the financial benefit (or saving) to the state is the difference between the costs of providing education using these two different types of inputs.

In the 1965–66 academic year the availability of T.A.'s permitted a reduction of nearly $2 million in California state funds for undergraduate instruction. This was possible because the average salary rate of full-time instructors at the University of California, $6,985 per academic year,[20] was $1,385 greater than the rate for full-time T.A.'s, around $5,600.[21] This $1,385 saving in the state instructional budget was realized for each of the 1,400 full-time T.A.'s.[22]

The $2 million annual savings produced by T.A.'s amounts to

[20] Coordinating Council for Higher Education, *Annual Report on Faculty Salaries, Benefits, and Recruitment,* No. 1023 (Sacramento, Calif., January, 1966), p. 22.

[21] Correspondence with Jerome Evans, Consultant, Joint Committee on Higher Education.

[22] *Ibid.* Actually, T.A.'s generally teach only half time and are paid accordingly.

2 percent of the roughly $100 million in instructional funds paid for out of state general funds. The $2 million is a far greater percentage of the state funds devoted to the *graduate* program, but we have been unable to determine the amount of such funds. In any case, it seems clear that any fiscal analysis of graduate education should not neglect the contribution of graduate students to the undergraduate teaching program and the budget for that program. Were it not for the low cost instructional services provided by T.A.'s, the state of California would require, as we have shown, $2 million of additional funds per year to run the undergraduate program in its present form.

These calculations could be replicated for research assistants, provided good information were available on the average salaries of people who might perform comparable duties. Since graduate students are presumably available at market wage rates below those of non-students of comparable quality,[23] faculty research is thus made less costly.

So far we have talked about the financial benefits from graduate training through the undergraduate instruction and faculty research routes. We have not, however, been able to estimate—for California—the additional lifetime incomes attributable to graduate education, as we did earlier for undergraduate education. There is no body of data for California indicating the size of the monetary payoff from graduate training which would permit the development of estimates comparable to those given in Table II-3.[24]

However, by way of illustration of what could be done, we have employed United States data to estimate the additional lifetime income that is associated with graduate education (five years or more of college) rather than only undergraduate education (four years). After reducing the differentials observed in the decennial census data by 25 percent—our rough adjustment factor for differential student ability—we find that an average male can expect

[23] University of California, *Financial Report,* Fiscal Year 1965–1966, p. 3.

[24] Some exploratory work has been done on the payoffs to professional training; see W. Lee Hansen, " 'Shortages' and Investment in Health Manpower," *The Economics of Health and Medical Care* (Ann Arbor: University of Michigan, 1964), pp. 75–91; B. W. Wilkinson, "Present Values of Lifetime Earnings for Different Occupations," *Journal of Political Economy,* LXXIV (December, 1966), pp. 556–73.

about $26,000 of additional lifetime income—having a present value of $5,800—as a result of his investment in graduate education.[25]

OTHER EFFECTS OF HIGHER EDUCATION

As noted at the beginning of this chapter, higher education produces a variety of effects other than the financial ones we have been discussing. These include consumption effects, external social effects, and external income effects. In contrast to our discussion of the financial effects, these are more difficult to measure. Thus, our discussion is of a qualitative rather than a quantitative nature.

CONSUMPTION EFFECTS. Higher education is valued for more than purely monetary reasons—the ability to earn a greater lifetime income. It is also valued because of its effect on the lives of those who have experienced the process. One cannot entirely separate the skills and knowledge obtained in school into skills applied to work and knowledge applied to cultural, social, political, and other areas of life. When a person works he is also a citizen, a neighbor, and a member of a family. The education he receives is broadly applied; it affects the whole range of his activities.

These consumption effects are not, however, confined to the period after graduation from college. Some of them are obtained during the period of schooling itself. While these effects are generally viewed as beneficial, the recent rising level of student tension— at least a part of which has been directed at universities and colleges—may suggest that changes in student attitudes, wrought, at least in part by education, are offering some of the consumption benefits of higher education.

EXTERNAL SOCIAL EFFECTS. While the consumption effects of higher education are undoubtedly considered by the individuals directly involved, we are also interested in the external social effects —those which accrue to others. To the extent that these effects are positive and sizable, the rationale for public subsidies for higher education is greatly strengthened. What are some of the major types of external social effects?

[25] The importance of this financial return is difficult to assess, however, since little is known about the average amount of time spent in graduate school by this group of census respondents, or about the costs of providing education to them.

Higher education appears to make important contributions to the quality of citizen and community responsibility. This is suggested by data such as those which show that the percentage of the population that votes increases with educational level. In one study of two recent Presidential elections, it was found that for both males and females, in the South and in the non-South, and at all ages, the percentage of persons who voted increased with the level of schooling. For example, among males age thirty-four to fifty-four, 80 percent of grade school graduates, 87 percent of high school graduates, and 96 percent of college graduates voted.[26] Similarly, education seems to develop a sense of citizen duty in people, as reflected by their attitudes toward government and their own involvement in the processes of government.[27]

Another socially beneficial effect of higher education is its presumed contribution to equality of opportunity. Education provides access to a wide range of options and opportunities that might otherwise be closed off to certain segments of our society. Of course, higher education is not the sole route to a more equitable society; other forms of human resource development, such as job training or even outright subsidies, may be equally or even more productive than higher education.[28] Moreover, the extent to which higher education actually does contribute may not be great, given the fact that children from poorer families are least likely to be admitted to higher education or, if admitted, to complete a four year program. (More detailed attention is given to this issue in Chapter IV.)

Although increased educational opportunities are beneficial for those who can avail themselves of them, the aggregate result of the increased educational attainments may be to widen the gulf in understanding between population groups (e.g., between the young and the old, whites and non-whites, rich and poor). The student demonstrations that have occurred in recent months have pointed up some of the consequences of differences in values and attitudes to which the higher education system itself may have directly con-

[26] A. Campbell and others, *The American Voter* (New York: John Wiley and Sons, Inc., 1960), Table 17-11, p. 495.

[27] Burton A. Weisbrod, *External Benefits of Public Education* (Princeton, N.J.: Industrial Relations Section, Princeton University, 1964), pp. 95–96.

[28] For some evidence on this issue, see W. Lee Hansen, Burton A. Weisbrod, and William J. Scanlon, "Determinants of Earnings: Does Schooling Really Count?" (University of Wisconsin, mimeo, 1968).

tributed. That some segments of society find this not to their liking is reflected in the financial and political pressures put upon state educational institutions in the aftermath of these demonstrations.

Another important class of external effects of education comes from the reduced transfer payments for welfare, unemployment compensation, and the like, which go heavily to the less educated. Presumably, with more education and the higher earning power it generates, there would be less need for such transfer payments. In this manner, taxpayers in general share in the real economic benefits—that is, share in the increased productivity—resulting from higher education. Thus, if some incremental expenditures on higher education were to increase earnings of the previously less educated by, say, $100 per period, and if, as a result, welfare or other transfer payments to these people were cut by $20 per period, then the $100 of increased earnings would be divided into $80 for those educated and $20 for taxpayers in general. The reduction in transfers (to the extent that it occurs) is not an *additional* benefit (additional to the increased total earnings); it is simply a *redistribution* of benefits.

Finally, there are the benefits produced for society through the discovery and application of new knowledge which results from research carried on by college and university faculties. It is certainly no easy task to separate the teaching and research functions, and this makes the identification of such returns difficult. It should be pointed out, however, that considerable amounts of the research performed by colleges and universities—and particularly those in California—are financed by the federal government; thus the benefits should be attributed to federal rather than to state expenditures. This does not deny, though, that were more state funds spent on research, greater external social benefits would undoubtedly result.

EXTERNAL INCOME EFFECTS. Among the external benefits frequently claimed for higher education are the effects on total income in the area. It is argued that the presence of a university attracts industry, research firms, and people. Let us examine this assertion.

To begin, it should be noted that if total income in the state is enhanced, there remains the question of what would happen if the state devoted additional money and resources to some purpose other than higher education; would the state be more or less attractive to industry and people if, instead of increasing spending for higher education, the state used the funds for other public services —parks, streets, sewers, etc.—or if it reduced taxes? The answer is not obvious, and this, we believe, is a significant observation. Increased spending for higher education may or may not be an efficient means—compared with the alternatives—for enhancing the economic attractiveness of an area.

Moreover, even if increased expenditures on higher education do increase income and employment in the immediate area, this does not imply that they increase income and employment for the state as a whole (and certainly not necessarily for the entire nation). Many of the favorable effects in the immediate area will come at the expense of other areas. Thus, gauging the favorable income effects of increased public expenditures in the area immediately affected can be a very misleading indicator of effects for the state as a whole.[29]

There is scant evidence, however, that the attractiveness of an area to business firms is actually very sensitive to the level of higher education expenditures. The frequently heard examples of research complexes in the Boston and San Francisco Bay areas have, in our judgment, served as the basis for quite unsupported generalizations about the great virtue of high quality higher education as an economic development measure. There are many factors influencing the location of firms, and although ease of access to a university faculty is one—at least for certain firms—there is little evidence that modest, or even substantial changes in a state's support for higher education produce significant effects on location of firms. There are, for example, many excellent universities in this country in communities which have attracted few, if any, research firms or other university related employers.

Throughout this discussion it should be borne in mind that we are not really considering the effects of having a university or a higher education system, but the effects of realistic *changes* in the level of financial support for it. The issue for California—or for any other state—is not whether to have such a system, but, rather, at what level (and in what form) to support it. Thus, with respect to the economic development issue we are now discussing, the question is whether *variations* in the level of state support would

[29] A special case is the impact of the spending of out-of-state students. For California higher education this is a relatively less important factor than in many states, since the proportion of out-of-state students is small. However, the increased consumption of public services acts to offset any spending effects of out-of-state students.

produce meaningful *changes* in business location decisions. In addition, it must be remembered that, in California, any additional spending would likely be spread over the many University campuses, not to mention the numerous State Colleges or even the Junior Colleges. Typically, however, the developmental effects of public higher education in the state are equated with the characteristics of a particular campus—Berkeley; this assumes that Berkeley exerts a very powerful, and, indeed, unrealistically high leverage effect.

Although we have indicated reservations about whether changes in expenditures on higher education would be expected to influence greatly an area's attractiveness to employers, and whether, if they did, the effects might not be greater if the funds were devoted to other public expenditure programs, or to reduced taxes, there remains another issue: how anxious should an area—or a state—be to attract employers and population? People and employers help generate income and taxes, but they also generate increased demand for public services. Thus, attracting people is not necessarily a sound objective of public policy.

To summarize this section: (a) Increased financial support for higher education may attract business and population, but so would other types of public expenditures, or reduced taxes. (b) The evidence that changes in the level of a state's support for higher education do have a significant effect on location decisions as among states is essentially non-existent. (c) There is a question as to the desirability of attracting still more population to a state such as California, which is already confronting problems resulting from rapid in-migration. Thus, the argument that increased support for higher education would produce external benefits through the economic development route must be seriously questioned.

Our apparent skepticism about either the existence or significance of some of the widely discussed external benefits from higher education stems principally from the absence of any substantial body of evidence in support of them. Indeed, much of the so-called evidence is anecdotal in nature. We do not, however, wish to assert that external benefits do not exist; only that they are elusive and demanding of a great deal of hard attention.

Chapter III

THE COSTS OF PUBLIC HIGHER
EDUCATION IN CALIFORNIA

What are the costs of public higher education? Costs may be viewed quite differently by students, by their parents, by taxpayers, and by those who take the viewpoint of society as a whole. Consider the latter perspective: real resources are used up in the process of producing higher education—resources capable of alternative uses. Thus, the real cost of higher education is the loss of the goods and services, or leisure, that must be given up to provide the fact that resource inputs are used in higher education. But these costs are shared—by taxpayers through the tax payments they make, and by parents and students through direct outlays as well as through the income that is foregone while students attend school.

What forms do the private and social costs of higher education take? What are their magnitudes for the California system of public higher education? How much of the costs is being borne by students and parents? By taxpayers? Which taxpayers? What are the effects, if any, of alternative means of sharing the costs? These are the principal questions addressed in this chapter.

EMPIRICAL ESTIMATES

Some light is shed on a number of these issues by Table III-1, which presents estimates on a per student basis of a number of forms of

TABLE III-1. AVERAGE COSTS OF EDUCATION AT UNIVERSITY
OF CALIFORNIA, BY TYPE OF COST, AND AMOUNTS BORNE
BY STUDENTS AND PARENTS, AND BY CALIFORNIA
TAXPAYERS, 1964–65

| | Lower Division Student | | |
	Total	*Amount Borne by Student and Parents*	*Amount Borne by California Taxpayers*
Cost Category			
1. Instructional	$ 709⎫	$ 250	$1,214
2. Capital	755⎭		
3. Books and Supplies	150	150	0
4. Foregone Earnings	2,000	2,000	0
Total, 1–4	$3,610 (100%)	$2,400 (66%)	$1,214 (34%)
5. Room, Board, and Transportation	500	500	0
Total, 1–5	$4,110 (100%)	$2,900 (71%)	$1,214 (29%)

| | Upper Division Student | | |
	Total	*Amount Borne by Student and Parents*	*Amount Borne by California Taxpayers*
Cost Category			
1. Instructional	$1,355⎫	$ 250	$1,860
2. Capital	755⎭		
3. Books and Supplies	150	150	0
4. Foregone Earnings	4,000	3,980	20
Total, 1–4	$6,260 (100%)	$4,380 (70%)	$1,880 (30%)
5. Room, Board, and Transportation	500	500	0
Total, 1–5	$6,760 (100%)	$4,880 (72%)	$1,880 (28%)

Sources: *Line 1:* CCHE, *Feasibility and Desirability of Eliminating Lower Division Programs at Selected Campuses of the University of California and the California State Colleges* (mimeo.), January 6, 1967, Table 18, p. 124. Based on data for 1963–64. Student and parents contributions from *Analysis of the Budget Bill of the State of California for the Fiscal Year, July 1, 1967 to June 30, 1968*, Report of the Legislative Analyst to the Joint Committee, Table 5, p. 290. *Line 2:* Total capital cost for each type of institution divided by its enrollment. (A) Capital costs from various sources. (1) California Legislature 1966. *Analysis of the Budget Bill 1966–67*, Items 107, 108 for UC and State Colleges. (2) State Controller, *Financial Transactions Concerning School Districts of California 1965–66*, Table 2. (B) Enrollment: *Total and Full Time Enrollment, California Institutions of Higher Education, Fall 1965*, pp. 11, 21, and 37. *Line 3:* College Entrance Examination Board, *Student Financial Aid Administration Requirements and Resources at the University of California*, Table 19, p. II-17. *Line 4:* Our estimates. *Line 5:* Edward Sanders and Hans Palmer, *The Financial Barriers to Higher Education in California* (Claremont: Pomona College, 1965), Table XIV, p. 216.

costs of education at the University of California. The instructional and capital cost categories reflect the various resource costs of teachers, facilities, and related inputs utilized per student. Ideally, we would want to know the amounts by which the total of these

TABLE III-2. AVERAGE COST OF EDUCATION AT CALIFORNIA STATE COLLEGES, BY TYPE OF COST, AND AMOUNTS BORNE BY STUDENTS AND PARENTS, AND BY CALIFORNIA TAXPAYERS, 1964–65

| | Lower Division Student | | |
	Total	Amount Borne by Student and Parents	Amount Borne by California Taxpayers
Cost Category			
1. Instructional	$ 578 ⎫	$ 100	$1,248
2. Capital	770 ⎭		
3. Books and Supplies	150	150	0
4. Foregone Earnings	2,000	2,000	0
Total, 1–4	$3,498 (100%)	$2,250 (64%)	$1,248 (36%)
5. Room, Board, and Transportation	450	450	0
Total, 1–5	$3,948 (100%)	$2,700 (68%)	$1,248 (32%)
	Upper Division Student		
	Total	Amount Borne by Student and Parents	Amount Borne by California Taxpayers
Cost Category			
1. Instructional	$ 781 ⎫	$ 100	$1,451
2. Capital	770 ⎭		
3. Books and Supplies	150	150	0
4. Foregone Earnings	4,000	3,980	20
Total, 1–4	$5,701 (100%)	$4,230 (74%)	$1,471 (26%)
5. Room, Board, and Transportation	450	450	0
Total, 1–5	$6,151 (100%)	$4,680 (76%)	$1,471 (24%)

Source: See Table III-1.

costs would rise (or fall) as a result of a given size increase (or decrease) in the permanent number of students. In practice, however, we can presently do no better than to estimate these *incremental* costs by the *average* cost now being incurred. Tables III-1 through III-3 show that the per student instructional and capital

TABLE III-3. AVERAGE COST OF EDUCATION AT CALIFORNIA
JUNIOR COLLEGES, BY TYPE OF COST, AND AMOUNTS
BORNE BY STUDENTS AND PARENTS, AND BY
CALIFORNIA TAXPAYERS, 1964–65

	Total	Amount Borne by Student and Parents	Amount Borne by California Taxpayers
Cost Category			
1. Instructional	$ 441 ⎫	$ 0	$721
2. Capital	280 ⎭		
3. Books and Supplies	150	150	0
4. Foregone Earnings	2,000	2,000	0
Total, 1–4	$2,871 (100%)	$2,150 (75%)	$721 (25%)
5. Room, Board, and Transportation	0	0	0
Total, 1–5	$2,871 (100%)	$2,150 (75%)	$721 (25%)

Source: See Table III-1.

costs differ among the three California systems of colleges and universities (University, State Colleges, and Junior Colleges), and differ also between lower division (first two years) and upper division (second two years).[1] The variation in these costs among the three systems is noteworthy, for as we shall see in greater detail later, these cost differences reflect differential levels of public subsidy. Resource costs (instructional plus capital) per student-year average $721 in a California Junior College, $1,348 in the lower division at a State College, and more than $2,100 in the upper division at a University of California campus.

These differences in costs reflect a multitude of factors as-

[1] For our purposes here we shall employ the definitions conventionally used within the California system of higher education. Instructional costs are usually defined clearly, though one might argue about the appropriateness of the definition. Instructional costs reflects some compensation for faculty research. A question might be raised about the legitimacy of allocating such research costs of "instruction" and, hence, about allowing these costs to be included in the estimates of subsidies. Although the research component of the instructional budget is difficult to estimate, the likelihood is that it is smallest, in absolute terms, at the Junior Colleges and largest at the University. Thus, the effect of excluding it would be to reduce the differences in "true" instructional costs per student-year among the three higher education systems.

There are also questions as to the appropriate measurements of capital costs as they relate to teaching programs. In any case, capital costs are generally ignored in determining the level of total instructional costs. Yet,

sociated in part at least with the quality of instruction and quality of education provided at each type of institution and at each level of instruction—differences in faculty quality (as indicated by the percent of the faculty having doctorates), in class size, in the number of books available in libraries at each institution, and in still other quality indicators.[2]

Tables III-1 through III-3 also show the direct contribution of students and parents to the instructional and capital costs. These contributions, which consist of student charges—incidental and related student fees—range from about $250 at the University to zero at the Junior Colleges.

The reality of the Books and Supplies category of cost is clear. But the next entry, Foregone Earnings, requires elaboration.[3] As we explained in Chapter I, a cost should be viewed as anything that is given up to attain some objective, whether or not any cash payment is involved. Since obtaining college education requires the student to be present in school, one form of cost of higher education is—from the student's point of view—the income that he could have earned were he to work full-time rather than attend school; and from society's point of view, that foregone income reflects output that is (at least temporarily) not produced, by virtue of the potential labor resource having been withdrawn from the labor market. The amount of foregone income (productivity) varies with the person's age, sex, and educational level, and so the amount of this cost differs between lower and upper divisions in Tables III-1, III-2, and III-3. We have assumed that foregone earnings are substantially higher at the upper division, reflecting in part the fact that foregone earnings should indicate the improved income opportunities afforded by the completion of two years of college.

---

in terms of the resources required to provide instruction an allowance should certainly be made for this important category of costs. Because capital costs are not normally calculated on a per student basis, we have had to make our own estimates. In doing so, capital costs are assumed to be equal for lower and upper division students.

[2] See CCHE, *Feasibility and Desirability of Eliminating Lower Division Programs at Selected Campuses of the University of California and the California State Colleges* (mimeo), January 6, 1967 (preliminary version).

[3] For additional discussions of costs, see T. W. Schultz, "Capital Formation by Education," *Journal of Political Economy*, LXVIII (December, 1960), 571–83; and Mary Jean Bowman, "The Costing of Human Resource Development," in E. A. G. Robinson and J. E. Vaizey (eds.), *The Economics of Education* (New York: St. Martins Press, 1966), pp. 421–50.

It is true that the foregone earnings cost is not an out-of-pocket cost, but it imposes, nonetheless, a financial sacrifice—particularly on low income families which might badly need the income that their college age sons or daughters could contribute through full-time work. There is reason to believe that this cost element discourages low income youngsters from attending college, although student financial aid does go some way toward counteracting this force.

The importance of foregone income may not be restricted to low income families, particularly when it is realized that the income may be foregone either by the student, by his parents, or by a combination of both. That is, although it would appear that a student loses income by attending college, he may be aided by his parents to such an extent that he is as well off as he would have been as a full-time worker. In this case, the student would have foregone no income whatsoever, the full burden being borne by his parents. Depending on how the cost burden of foregone income is shared between students and their parents, the willingness of young people to attend college is likely to be affected.

Finally, line 5 covers a familiar cost category of room, board, and transportation, though these costs are treated in a manner that may be less familiar. The appropriate cost concept is not the *total* charge for, or the total cost of providing, housing and food for a student. It is instead the difference between the cost of providing these services at school and the cost of providing them at home, or wherever else the student would otherwise live. For students living at home the *additional* room and board (and transportation) cost associated with college education is essentially zero; for students living away from home the additional cost is estimated at about one-half of the room and board charge—or about $500 at the University and $450 at the State Colleges.[4]

Our objective in presenting Tables III-1, III-2, and III-3 is two-

[4] The cost figures—$500 for University of California students and $450 for State College students—are taken from Edward Sanders and Hans Palmer, *The Financial Barriers to Higher Education in California* (Claremont: Pomona College, 1965), Table XIV, p. 216. These are only slightly higher than more recent estimates of the CEEB and State Colleges. See *Financial Aid Administration Requirements and Resources at the University of California,* Table 19, p. II-7. Also, "California State Colleges Statement," *Tuition for California's Public Institutions of Higher Education,* Joint Committee on Higher Education Hearings, October 13 and 16, 1967.

fold: to show the principal forms and magnitudes of higher education costs, and to show how those costs are shared between students
and parents, on one hand, and taxpayers, on the other.[5] The matter
of cost-sharing is generally discussed in terms of the instructional
and capital costs of public higher education, but we suggest that
this is an excessively narrow focus. There are other costs, and the
question of how they are shared is no less important—either in
terms of equity or economic efficiency—than is the sharing of the
instructional and capital costs.

There has been much discussion of whether it is equitable
(though not whether it is economically efficient) for taxpayers to
pay so large a fraction of cost, given the expectation of sizable
financial benefits to students during their working lifetimes. We
cannot resolve disagreements resulting from differences in value
judgments as to what is equitable, but we can point out that the
cost-sharing picture appears vastly different depending on whether
one looks only at the sharing of instructional and capital costs, or
at the sharing of total costs.[6]

[5] It should be noted that the figures presented here differ from those
shown in CCHE, *Financial Assistance Programs* (2d rev., October 31, 1967),
Table I-1. The differences arise primarily in the treatment of instructional
and capital costs and in the treatment of foregone income. With respect to
the first, we have used what we feel to be more appropriate definitions of
instructional costs, capital costs, and enrollments. With respect to the treatment of foregone income, the CCHE report disregards this, using instead a
figure for "subsistence costs" that is not only lower than foregone income
but, in our judgment, not relevant conceptually.

[6] If the cost figures in this section are compared with the income benefits
in Chapter II, the rates of return on California higher education may be
estimated. For example, data in Table III-2 (page 43) indicate that the cost
of a four-year education at a California State College is $3948 for each of the
first two years and $6151 for each of the last two, for a total cost of approxi-
mately $20,200. In present value terms, as of age 18, and using a 5 percent
discount rate, the total costs fall to about $18,500. Since the present value of
income benefits (also at a 5 percent discount rate) for a male, college graduate is some $20,900 (Table II-3, page 22), it is clear that our figures imply an
internal rate of return of slightly more than 5 percent. This is less than the
approximately 10 percent that has been found in most other studies (for example, Giora Hanoch, "An Economic Analysis of Earnings and Schooling,"
Journal of Human Resources, II (Summer, 1967), pp. 310–329, especially
page 322). Our estimate does reflect, however, an adjustment for "ability"
which apparently was not made in the study cited. Without this adjustment
our estimated rate of return would have been between 7 and 8 percent.

PROPORTION OF COSTS BORNE
BY STUDENTS AND THEIR FAMILIES

When all forms of cost are taken into account, two important conclusions—both relevant to public policy decisions—follow: First,
as we observed above, the total cost of attending college is far in
excess of any student charges for fees and tuition; second, the fraction of *total* costs borne by students and their families is far greater
than the fraction borne by taxpayers through state and local support for higher education, at least in California. Table III-1, for
example, shows that for a lower division student living at home, the
total costs of his higher education are about $3,600 per year, of which
two-thirds is borne by the student and his family. For students living
away from home—roughly 30 percent of all University of California
students—the total cost of their education is about $4,100, more than
70 percent of which is borne by the student and his family.

Cast in this light, it becomes clear that although students and
parents now pay only $250 toward the nearly $1,500 average cost of
instruction and capital—about 15 percent—they bear a total burden,
before considering student aid, not of $250 but of $2,400 to $2,900!
From a state's fiscal point of view the important fact remains that
taxpayers now pay about 85 percent of instructional and capital
costs, and students and their families pay only 15 percent. However,
from a broader point of view it is important to note—both with
respect to equity and to effects of cost on college-going—that students and parents pay two-thirds or more of *total* costs. Of course,
these figures change as we consider the upper division costs, as
shown in the lower portion of Table III-1.

Actually, students and parents pay even more than these tables
indicate. We pointed out earlier that the additional state and local
taxes paid out of the increased earnings of college educated people
amount to $1,000 in present value terms for male college graduates
(Table II-3), and $700 for females (Table II-7). For males this is
an average of $250 per year of college—an amount which should
be added to the student contribution shown in Tables III-1, III-2,
and III-3. The effect of this addition is to raise to 76 percent the portion of total upper division costs at the University of California that
is eventually paid by students and their families.

A comparison of data in Tables III-1, III-2, and III-3 discloses
that there are marked differences in costs between lower and upper
divisions, and among the three California systems. Although these

differences result in part from the fact that instructional costs and capital costs differ by system and between lower and upper division within each system, an important factor is the difference in fore-gone earnings for lower and upper divisions.

COSTS OF LIVING AWAY
FROM HOME AND STUDENT AID

The analysis above has recognized that living on campus rather than at home entails additional costs. Our tables have indicated that these costs are borne by students and parents, but this is not entirely correct. Some of the additional costs incurred by students living away from home are borne by taxpayers through the student aid budget. The general point is that the need for student aid—as that need is currently measured—depends on the student's total costs, in-cluding the additional cost of living away from home, if the student does so. It has not been possible to determine how much of the additional costs associated with living away from home are actually being paid by taxpayers through student aid. We are able, how-ever, to estimate the amount of added *need* for student aid that is attributable to students at the University of California who live away from home.

Before discussing this estimate, it is worth pointing out that students often have the choice of attending a local college as a commuter or attending another institution as a resident—with dif-ferent cost implications for the public treasury. Similarly, society (government) has the choice of locating campuses within or very near population centers, which would obviously facilitate access by commuters, or of locating campuses in less accessible spots, where commuting is far less feasible. Society also has the choice of granting or not granting additional aid to those students who choose not to live at home when they could do so.

Is it the case that a significant portion of the needed student financial aid results from additional living costs? At the University of California it is estimated that room and board on campus ex-ceeds home maintenance by $500 per academic year.[7] The effect

[7] College Entrance Examination Board (CEEB), *Student Financial Aid Administration Requirements and Resources at the University of California* (1967), Vol. I, Table 19, II-17. The $450 figure assumes that resident students would have transportation costs associated with travel to and from home approximately equal to the commuting costs of a student living at

of this cost difference can be seen by looking at the level of support that the University expects will be provided by parents with different income levels. Assume that University students contribute $400 (through their own earnings) towards their education, that representative expenses for a student residing on campus are $1,850, that expenses for a commuting student are $1,400, and that no financial aid is provided. Under these assumptions, parents of resident students would be required to contribute an amount of $1,450 and parents of commuting students an amout of $1,000.

According to the College Entrance Examination Board (CEEB) analysis, a parental contribution of $1,000 should not be expected from families with income less than $10,000, while a contribution of $1,450 should not be expected until family income reaches $12,000.[8] Thus, if parental incomes exceed $12,000, no financial aid should be given on the basis of need, regardless of where the student lives. If parental income falls between $10,000 and $12,000, however, the student would qualify for financial aid if he chose to live on campus but not if he lived at home. If parental income is below $10,000 he qualifies for financial aid in any case, but he would receive more aid if he lived on campus. Thus, for each student in a family with less than $12,000 annual income, a decision to live on campus leads to an increase in the amount of financial aid for which he is eligible.

The CEEB study shows that 11,313, or 48.4 percent, of all unmarried students who reside on the University campuses come from families with incomes less than $12,500.[9] If these students were to live at home and commute, the total amount of financial aid required would be reduced by approximately $450 per student, which, for the 11,000 students involved, would amount to more than $5 million annually. A comparison of this figure with the total financial aid budget for the University—approximately $13.7 million in 1966–67—shows clearly that the policy issue of encouragement or discouragement of on-campus residence is a significant one.

---

home. However, if the student lives close enough to commute but prefers to live on campus this assumption would not be accurate. Here we use a more recent estimate of the cost differential, to relate our discussion better to the CEEB financial aid analysis.

[8] *Ibid.*, Vol. I, Table 12, p. II-8. We have assumed a family with three dependent children in assessing the family contribution.

[9] *Ibid.*, Vol. II, Table 5, p. G-10. Based on spring quarter enrollment, 1967. In this table the $12,500 income break was closest to the $12,000 income cutoff in the CEEB data.

Further, the CEEB has estimated that the University's need for financial aid was $4.8 million more than the $13.7 million that was actually available to undergraduates.[10] Thus, in relation to either the expenditures for student aid or the estimated need, the $5 million sum shown above to result from additional on-campus living costs is large indeed. We see that $5 million out of a total needed of $18.5 million, or 27 percent of the total estimated financial need, can be attributed to room and board costs for non-commuters.

We definitely do not intend to imply that, simply because there are public costs associated with the present policies of campus location and of free choice by students as to whether to live at home, the current policies are necessarily bad. Alternatives involving more or less commuting may be even more costly, in terms of monetary costs or educational values or both. But we do want to make clear that the cost implications of present policies are not unimportant.

COSTS OF COLLEGE ATTENDANCE BY FAMILY INCOME LEVELS

We have no good body of information on how the cost elements just discussed vary by family income among California students. In the absence of such data, we shall speculate about what these cost patterns might look like.

Instructional and capital costs are incurred by the institutions of higher education and thus are independent of student-parental income levels. The same will be true of student charges, except for fee remissions. Similarly, books and supplies are likely to cost about the same for all students. This leaves only foregone income and incremental living costs as having much potential for variation. To the extent that job access is in part related to family position, we would expect foregone incomes to be positively related to family income. Incremental living costs would also be positively associated with family income, reflecting the fact that larger percentages of low income students will live at home where costs are lower.

The only data specifically available for California are the CEEB data on University of California students. This study assumes a uniform out-of-pocket cost of $1,850 per school year (based on attendance for three quarters) regardless of income level; this

[10] *Ibid.*, Vol. I, p. xv.

figure reflects room and board, student charges, incidental travel, books and supplies, and the like.[11] (Of course, there are variations, principally between commuters and those living away from home, as already noted.) The finding of constancy of living costs across income levels is consistent with the finding in a study of students at the University of Wisconsin.[12] While student expenditures did rise slightly at the very highest income levels, they were relatively invariant otherwise.

The point of this discussion is to indicate that the total costs as well as students' costs are not closely related to family income. Thus, the level of costs poses a substantially greater financial barrier to low income students.

Against this relative constancy of costs there are several off-setting factors, namely, variations in student financial aid—grants and loans—and in student earnings. Grants and loans go in relatively larger amounts to low income students than to others. But, the amounts of aid granted are generally small relative to total student costs and therefore serve in only a small way to offset the financial barriers to college attendance by low income students. Student earnings are a more important source of support across all family income levels, though the pressures to work during the school year appear to be far greater among the low income group students.

While earning one's way through college, or at least providing a substantial portion of one's support, has long been regarded as exemplary, little is known about how the diversion of this time detracts from the many intellectual, cultural, and social pursuits that non-working students can avail themselves of. If outside work does seriously impede the educational process and thereby reduces the potential benefits to be derived from higher education, a fundamental rethinking of financial aid programs is in order.

TUITION AS A PROPORTION
OF REAL COST TO STUDENT

In viewing the costs of higher education from the student-parent standpoint, our discussion in this chapter has another implication.

[11] *Ibid.*, Vol. II, Table 3, Appendix E, p. 5.

[12] L. Joseph Lins, Allan P. Abell, and David R. Stucki, *Costs of Attendance and Income of Madison Campus Students: the University of Wisconsin, 1964-65 Academic Year* (Office of Institution Studies, University of Wisconsin, Madison, Wisconsin, January, 1967), p. 69.

At public universities where student charges are relatively low, these charges (including tuition and fees) constitute a rather inconsequential portion of the real cost to the student-parent unit of having a son or daughter go to college. With a foregone income cost of perhaps $2,000 per year, books and supplies cost of $150, and, frequently, additional room and board costs of $500, not to mention fees of some $250 per year—for a total of nearly $3,000 annually— the tuition issue loses much of its quantitative significance. A doubling of student charges—whether through tuition or increased fees—would amount to less than a 10 percent increase in the total cost to a family of sending a son or daughter to college.

This does not mean that student charges are unimportant in influencing which of several alternative colleges or universities a student attends, or whether a given person attends college at all. For low income families in particular, even a 10 percent increase can pose an important and perhaps insurmountable barrier to college attendance. The main point is that emphasis on the tuition rate or on student fees is misguided if one's objective is to provide equality of access to higher education, regardless of family circumstances.

From this standpoint, attention should be focused instead on total costs and on means for helping needy students finance them. Negative student charges—that is, sizable outright grants, particularly to offset the foregone income—may even be required as the lower reaches of family income are approached.

Evidence of the overall effect of student charges, or changes in them, on the number of students attending colleges is virtually nonexistent. Nor is much known about the degree to which students-parents are influenced in the choice of college by the level of student charges. One recently published study, based on data for the United States over the last decade or so, estimates that a 10 percent increase in student charges was associated with approximately a 4 percent decrease in the number of students.[13] We would expect, though, that if a single university increased its charges the response would be greater as students shifted to other institutions. The magnitude of such a shift would depend critically on how easy it was to find a satisfactory and accessible substitute school. The task of making estimates of enrollment responses in California is complicated by the fact that there exist three different public systems, in addition to many private colleges within California. Thus, the opportunities for

[13] Robert Campbell and B. N. Siegel, "Demand for Higher Education in the United States," *American Economic Review*, LVII (June, 1967), 482–94.

the shift of students among schools in response to changes in student charges in any one system are substantial.

Our discussion of the costs of public higher education in California has led to consideration of the responsiveness of demand for higher education to changes in student charges. The connection between the level of educational costs, the level of student charges, and the level of student enrollments is a significant one. Decisions on how the costs should be shared affect student charges, which in turn affect enrollments. Therefore, the issue of *equity* in setting student charges (or, more broadly, in determining how total costs should be shared) is intertwined with the issue of *economic efficiency*—how many and which young people obtain what quantity and quality of higher education.

Chapter IV

DISTRIBUTION OF BENEFITS AND COSTS OF PUBLIC HIGHER EDUCATION IN CALIFORNIA

In an era of sharply rising costs of higher education, growing demands upon available public funds, and an increased emphasis on assuring equal educational opportunities, greater attention is being given than ever before to the question: Who should pay? In particular, questions have been raised as to whether the financial contribution of *taxpayers* should be larger or smaller than it now is, with an offsetting change in the amount paid by parents and students.

Many elements are relevant in considering these questions. The principal ones are: the extent to which the subsidy provided through public higher education—via below-cost student charges—is widely available; and the extent to which the costs of providing this subsidy are or are not shared among taxpayers. In this chapter, then, we shall provide some perspective on the combined distribution of subsidies and the taxes paid to support them, both among different citizen groups and among families at various income levels.

There are at least two quite different ways of approaching this topic. One method is to consider the extent to which the individual beneficiaries of higher education repay the public subsidies they receive through taxes assessed on the additional lifetime earnings attributable to their higher education. With the information presented in Chapters II and III we can present some rough calculations on this point. One difficulty with this approach is that while it may indicate the extent to which individuals pay or do not repay their subsidy via taxes, it gives little insight into the decision-making process regarding the current allocation of funds to higher education.

To remedy this, a second method can be employed. We can examine the current amount and distribution of higher education subsidies in conjunction with the distribution of tax payments for higher education made by the families of the subsidized students. Just as determinations must be made with respect to which young people are eligible for higher education subsidies, decisions must also be made as to how the current costs of these subsidies are to be distributed among taxpayers. The latter decision involves all citizens —whether educated or not and irrespective of whether their children are currently enrolled in higher education, were previously enrolled, or may enroll in the future. The fact that the decision-makers may not be aware that they are deciding such an all-inclusive distributional question does not make the matter any less crucial.

This general approach to the financing of higher education quite clearly makes taxpayers in general—the older generation— provide, through the state, direct financial assistance via below-cost student charges to the younger generation (or at least a portion of it). This approach to finance is predicated on two major assumptions. First, since young people and their parents are often neither in a good position to pay the full costs of education nor to finance it by borrowing against future earnings, society underwrites a share of these costs. The idea is that subsidy receivers, after the completion of their schooling, will repay society through the tax contribution they make, to the support of ever new groups of students. Second, it is generally assumed that the external effects produced by education make everyone better off, thereby justifying general tax support. Moreover, the subsidy itself helps to induce the acquisition of more education, so that these external benefits do indeed result. But these underlying assumptions can be questioned on several grounds.

First, not all young people are equally qualified or interested in pursuing higher education, nor are they equally able to finance it.

Thus, the subsidy is selective—rationed out on the basis of academic ability and performance, both of which are correlated with family income levels. Many taxpayers are therefore contributing to the support of higher education even though they, through their children, will receive no direct benefit. This is especially true for two groups: the many people who desire to attend private colleges, whether in California or elsewhere, and those who are neither interested in nor qualified to attend college.

Second, knowledge of the magnitudes of the external effects produced by higher education is exceedingly limited, as was pointed out in Chapter II. Therefore the rationale for generalized support is, at best, not clear cut.

Third, the private monetary gains may themselves be attractive enough to induce many people to obtain higher education, irrespective of the extent of external effects. If this is the case, subsidies will be unnecessary for many individuals.

To resolve these issues we must know more about the extent to which the families that pay the subsidies are the ones who benefit from them. In this chapter we consider first the lifetime repayment approach. We take up subsequently the more complex analysis of the current distribution of subsidies received and taxes paid, focusing on the situation existing in 1965.

THE LIFETIME APPROACH

The average male receiving a college education in California can expect, based on 1965 income and tax patterns, to repay through state and local taxes approximately $4,200 of the $89,000 of added lifetime income he will receive (Table II-3, line 5). When we convert this to a present value basis, these taxes amount to approximately $1,000.

How much of a public subsidy does the average male graduating from a California public institution receive? On the assumption that average instructional costs for undergraduates at the University of California approximate $700 at the lower division and over $1,350 at the upper division, with capital costs averaging $750, the public subsidy over four years equals $7,100.[1] When expressed in present

[1] See Tables III-1, III-2, and III-3 (of Chapter III above) for data used in this section. However, we interpret the subsidy as being the full amount

value terms, using a 5 percent discount factor, the total is scaled down to about $6,200. Were we to think of a person as undertaking two years of Junior College and then switching to one of the State Colleges—the most economical combination available to him—the present value of these costs would drop considerably, to approximately $4,400. For males completing one to three years of college (for which we shall assume an average of two years of college completed), the present value of the subsidy ranges from $1,810 for Junior College attendance to $2,700 for University of California attendance.

We can now contrast the present value of the subsidy received at the time the education is provided with the present value of the additional state and local taxes paid in subsequent years. As shown in Table IV-1, the present values of these subsidies range

TABLE IV-1. ESTIMATED PRESENT VALUES OF HIGHER
EDUCATION SUBSIDY AND OF ADDITIONAL STATE AND
LOCAL TAXES PAID BASED ON 5 PERCENT
DISCOUNT RATE

	(1) Present Value of Subsidy	(2) Present Value of Additional State and Local Taxes Paid	Present Value of Difference (1)–(2)
Educational Attainment			
Male College Graduates	$4,400 to 6,200	$1,000	$3,400 to 5,200
Males With Some College (Non-Graduates)	1,810 to 2,700	200	1,610 to 2,500

Source: Column 1: Based on data from Tables III-1, III-2, and III-3. Column 2: Based on data from Tables II-3 and II-6.

from roughly $4,400 to $6,200 for males obtaining degrees. The present value of the average additional later tax payment is, by contrast, $1,000. For those with some college, the subsidies range from $1,810 to $2,700, with the additional taxes of $200.

Though rough, these results provide important insights into the relationships between subsidies and the added taxes later ac-

of instructional and capital costs, inasmuch as we want to divorce our discussion from student aid, as seen in its widest sense, i.e., anything that reduces student costs, including student fees.

cruing to the state and local governments from the education they helped to provide. It is important to note that in no case do state and local taxpayers recoup the full value of the subsidy, at least not at the 5 percent discount rate. (They would, of course, recoup even less at higher discount rates.) State and local governments do even less well in recouping from those who receive some college education (two years, on average) but who do not graduate. Both the subsidy and the additional taxes paid are smaller than for college graduates. But because the impact on income of two years of college is proportionately less than for those who graduate, the relationship between subsidies received by students and the taxes repaid is less favorable.[2]

In summary, whether a student graduates from a four-year public college or completes less than four years, the additional lifetime taxes he pays have a present value which averages less than the higher-education subsidy he received. We want to caution against taking these results at face value and basing policy directly upon them. The underlying data on the income to Californians with varying amounts of education, the estimated tax payments, and the cost data are all rough.

Before going on, we might return briefly to consider the value we should impute to external and consumer benefits which were discussed in Chapter II. Here we can approach the issue in a slightly different manner, by inquiring how great these benefits would have to be, in order that when added to the present value of additional state and local taxes paid, the total would equal the present value of the subsidy. The answer is that the present value of external and consumer benefits would have to be between three and five times the present value of taxes paid for each public college graduate; and, for those with some public college education, between eight and twelve times—as can be deduced by comparing column 3 with column 2 in Table IV-1. Whether the value of external and consumption benefits at the state and local level reach such magnitudes is, at present, a matter for conjecture.

With regard to external benefits, there is no reason to view them only at the state and local level. Through the federal tax system,

[2] It should be pointed out that the results in Table IV-1 stem in part from the effects of outmigration and mortality. Were it not for these factors, the figures in column 2 would be approximately twice as large. Nevertheless there would remain a substantial excess of subsidy over taxes in column 3.

through migration, and in other ways, higher education affects people generally, whether they reside in California or not. As observed from Tables II-3 and II-6, for example, taxpayers across the nation benefit from the increased federal taxes paid, even though they provide no direct contribution to California's support for higher education.

Hence, we now shift to a national point of view, by comparing the present value of California subsidies for higher education with the present value of *all* additional taxes paid. As shown in Table IV-2, the correspondence between all additional taxes paid and the

TABLE IV-2. ESTIMATED PRESENT VALUES OF HIGHER
EDUCATION SUBSIDY AND OF ADDITIONAL FEDERAL,
STATE, AND LOCAL TAXES PAID, BASED ON A
5 PERCENT DISCOUNT RATE

	(1) Present Value of Subsidy	(2) Present Value of Additional Federal, State, and Local Taxes Paid	Present Value of Difference (1)–(2)
Educational Attainment			
Male College Graduates	$4,400 to 6,200	$4,800	$ – 400 to 1,400
Males With Some College			
(Non-Graduates)	1,810 to 2,700	900	910 to 1,800

Source: Same as Table IV-1.

subsidies received is much closer than it is for state and local taxes alone, at least for college graduates. Indeed, those going to the Junior College for two years and completing their work at the State Colleges—and thus receiving a $4,400 subsidy—on average repay $400 more than the subsidy. But there is still a substantial excess of subsidies over taxes for other college graduates as well as for those who do not complete college.

This analysis is of relevance when considering ways to finance public higher education. As shown here, while the national society at large benefits monetarily in a substantial way from California's public outlays on higher education, the share of these benefits received by Californians is far less than the contribution they make. Much the same situation holds when we consider that the Junior Colleges, heavily supported by local property taxes, yield benefits to other communities through migration within and without the state and concurrently distribute a share of the benefits via state taxes to all Californians.

While some might interpret these findings as implying the desirability of higher student charges—at least for those who can afford them—a more global view suggests a shifting of substantial responsibility for financing public higher education to the federal government. This is simply in recognition of which level of government gains most handsomely through its tax structure.

THE CROSS SECTION APPROACH [3]

We shift our attention now from the extent to which individual Californians receiving public higher education repay via higher lifetime taxes the subsidy they receive to consider the distribution by family income level of subsidies and taxes paid in a single year.

The public higher education system in the United States provides—or, at least, offers—a public subsidy to young people of college age. The extent to which the young people actually receive the subsidies depends on whether they can qualify for admission, whether they avail themselves of the opportunity to attend, and, if they do, what quantity and quality of education they receive. As a result, the amount of subsidy received through the public financing of higher education varies greatly from one person to another. Our objective in the balance of this chapter is to estimate the amounts of subsidies received through higher education, the variation in subsidies received by students depending upon the amount of schooling and the kind of schooling they obtain, and the extent to which these subsidies are received in different amounts by students whose families are at different socio-economic levels.[4]

Attention is restricted to undergraduate education, and the data used are for public education in California. While higher educational systems differ among states, it would appear that the results for California are broadly characteristic of those for a number of other states.

A knowledge of the magnitude and distribution of subsidies or

[3] A somewhat modified version of parts of this chapter appeared as "The Distribution of Costs and Direct Benefits of Public Higher Education: The Case of California," *Journal of Human Resources*, IV (Spring, 1969), 176–191.

[4] Little attention seems to have been given to this subject. For an interesting and perceptive foray, see Christopher Jencks, "Social Stratification and Mass Higher Education," *Harvard Education Review* (Spring, 1968).

direct benefits provided through public higher education, or indeed, through any public program, is important for what it suggests concerning appropriate pricing, tax, and expenditure policy. By appropriate we mean policies that will be efficient, in the sense of doing the most to raise output, and at the same time equitable, in the sense of doing the most to achieve society's distribution goals, such as providing greater equality of opportunity for young people. We can illustrate some of the possibilities. For those eligible for higher education, uniform subsidies may provide a windfall to the more financially able while doing little to facilitate college attendance by the less well-off. This might argue for some kind of flexible pricing system in higher education, though much the same effect could be achieved less directly through the tax system. For those not eligible for public higher education, the provision of other kinds of subsidies or direct benefit programs may not only yield substantial societal benefits, but also help to achieve greater equality, not only of educational opportunity but of opportunity in general.

SUBSIDIES STUDENTS CAN RECEIVE. The amounts of public higher education subsidies that can be received by college students are determined largely by the costs—instructional and capital—of providing instruction to them. However, the number of years the instruction is received is also relevant. Table IV-3 indicates how the amount of subsidies received will differ, given various assumed patterns of progression through the educational system in California —a state which, like many others, has three different higher education sub-systems. In the first two lines the annual as well as the cumulative subsidy for four years of undergraduate training at the University of California is shown, aggregating to $7,140 for a four year program. In the next four lines comparable information is shown for each of the other two public systems of higher education in California. In the California State College system a four year program would yield a subsidy of $5,800. The Junior College subsidy amounts to $1,440—this compares with $2,700 for the first two years at the State Colleges and $2,920 for the first two years at the University of California. These estimated subsidies at each of the three system are the sums of average instructional and capital costs per student.[5]

Because there is considerable movement of students among

[5] For additional detail and sources see Tables III-1, III-2, and III-3, above.

TABLE IV-3. PUBLIC HIGHER EDUCATION SUBSIDIES, BY TYPE OF PROGRAM
AND YEARS OF COLLEGE COMPLETED, 1965

Type of Program		Year of College			
		1	2	3	4
University of California—4 Years	Per Year Cost	$1,460	$1,460	$2,110	$2,110
	Cumulative Cost	1,460	2,920	5,030	7,140
State Colleges—4 Years	Per Year Cost	1,350	1,350	1,550	1,550
	Cumulative Cost	1,350	2,700	4,250	5,800
Junior Colleges—2 Years	Per Year Cost	720	720	—	—
	Cumulative Cost	720	1,440	—	—
Junior College—2 Years, and University of California—2 Years	Per Year Cost	$ 720	$ 720	$2,110	$2,110
	Cumulative Cost	720	1,440	3,550	5,660
State College—2 Years, and University of California—2 Years	Per Year Cost	1,350	1,350	2,110	2,110
	Cumulative Cost	1,350	2,700	4,810	6,920
University of California—2 Years, and State College—2 Years	Per Year Cost	1,460	1,460	1,550	1,550
	Cumulative Cost	1,460	2,920	4,470	6,020

Source: Based on Tables III-1, III-2, and III-3. The offset to instructional and capital costs provided through student fees is omitted, for the reason noted in the text.

the three segments of the entire system, we have also attempted to show how these subsidies will vary, based on several assumed patterns of transfer from one type of institution to another. Lines 7 and 8 show the subsidy resulting from a two year Junior College program followed by two years at the University of California; Lines 9 and 10 assume a two year State College system program followed by transfer to the University of California; and Lines 11 and 12 assume a two year program at the University of California, followed by transfer to the State College system for the final two years. The total subsidies involved in these latter three cases amount to $5,660, $6,920, and $6,020, respectively.

The import of this table should be clear. For those people completing a four year program a subsidy of more than $7,100 can be received—but only by those students who qualify, on the basis of their high school records, for the University of California. Those who do not qualify can obtain a maximum subsidy of $5,800 at the State Colleges. And for those eligible only for the Junior Colleges the maximum is $1,440, on the assumption that they do not later qualify for transfer to the State College system or the University of California. Therefore, depending upon one's ability level as determined by high school performance, the maximum amount of subsidy that can be received is fairly well determined.

SUBSIDIES STUDENTS DO RECEIVE. In reality, the matter is even more complex because not all students proceed through an entire four year course. A sizable number of students drop out at the end of each year, some for academic reasons and others for a variety of personal reasons. Thus, not everyone can or does choose to avail himself of the full amount of the subsidy for which he is potentially qualified. Equally important, there are others who, through lack of interest in public higher education, receive no subsidy whatsoever. These are people who join the work force immediately, enter military service, decide not to go on to college for other reasons, or enroll in private colleges.

The actual distribution of subsidies received by students entering each of the various segments of higher education in California is rather difficult to determine, given the paucity of data on attrition and transfer patterns. On the basis of fragmentary data, however, the approximate patterns of progression are indicated in Table IV-4.

It is quite clear that attrition at the Junior College level is by far the highest, reflecting the fact that a number of its programs require only one year of schooling; that for some students Junior College provides a stepping stone to a State College or University

TABLE IV-4. ESTIMATED PROGRESSION PATTERNS THROUGH PUBLIC HIGHER EDUCATION SYSTEMS IN CALIFORNIA, 1965

	Percentage of Freshmen Entrants in Each System Completing Indicated Year of Work								
	UC[a] System			SC[b] System			JC[c] System		
		Transfer to			Transfer to			Transfer to	
	Non-Transfer	SC	JC	Non-Transfer	UC	JC	Non-Transfer	UC	SC
Year of Work									
1	85	—	—	80	—	—	70	—	—
2	70	5	—	60	—	—	30	—	—
3	60	4	—	55	8	—	—	2	8
4	55	3	—	50	6	—	—	2	6

Source: Based on a variety of published and unpublished data on patterns of student progression and transfer, as well as on oral conversations with experts on this subject. Subsequent to the preparation of this table and the analysis upon which it is based, we came upon some additional data on transfer patterns among systems; see CCHE, *Feasibility and Desirability of Eliminating Lower Division Programs at Selected Campuses of the University of California and the California State Colleges* (mimeo), January 6, 1967 (this is a preliminary version of the report). The difference between the actual and our estimated patterns of transfer appear to be relatively minor and do not affect the general conclusions we have drawn.

  [a] University of California.
  [b] State College.
  [c] Junior College.

campus; and that for others, Junior Colleges serve the important function of giving young people a chance to survey the opportunities better before rushing into a job choice.

The rate of attrition at the State Colleges is somewhat lower, and attrition at the University of California is the lowest, largely as a result of its greater selectivity in admissions. Its first year attrition rate—15 percent—seems rather high, but the four year completion rate of 55 percent is within the range for most other comparable four year institutions. However, an additional three percent of the initial entrants to the University of California completed their work at a State College, and some others undoubtedly graduated

from colleges outside the California system of public higher education.

What can we now say about the distribution of the subsidies to
students eligible to enter each of the three different systems? The
data in Table IV-5 attempt to answer this question by showing
the distribution of all high school graduates by the percent who
are eligible and who say they plan to enroll or not enroll at each
type of college. The results of this table are interesting in a number
of respects.

TABLE IV-5. ESTIMATED DISTRIBUTION OF ALL HIGH SCHOOL
GRADUATES BY ELIGIBILITY FOR HIGHER EDUCATION AND
BY TYPE OF HIGHER EDUCATION THEY PLAN TO OBTAIN

	Plans to Attend by Type of Higher Education					
	UC	SC	JC	Other	None	All
Eligibility						
University of California	5%	4%	5%	3%	2%	19%
State Colleges	—	2	8	2	4	17
Junior Colleges	—	—	33	4	27	64
All	5%	6%	46%	9%	33%	100%

Source: Based on Coordinating Council for Higher Education, *Financial Assistance
Programs*, No. 67-13 (rev., October 31, 1967), Tables I-2 and I-3, pp. I-9 and I-10.

Consider the column labeled All, on the far right: only 19 percent of California high school seniors are eligible for the University
of California system, about 17 percent more are eligible for the
State College system, and the remaining 64 percent qualify only for
the Junior Colleges.[6] However, the distribution of students by
enrollment plans differs rather substantially, as indicated by the
bottom row labeled All. This shows that 5 percent of all graduating
high school students plan to go to the University of California (a
fourth of those eligible), 6 percent plan to enter the State College
system, 46 percent plan to enroll at Junior Colleges, 9 percent expect to enroll in private or out-of-state institutions, while 33 percent plan not to enroll in any college.

The extent to which students do not avail themselves of the
opportunity to go to the highest quality (highest subsidy) college
or university segment open to them is indicated by reading across

[6] Note that these figures differ somewhat from other data on eligibility,
as indicated by the Master Plan, for example.

each of the rows. Although 19 percent of all students are eligible for the University of California, only 5 percent plan to enroll at a University campus, with 4 percent going to State Colleges, 5 percent to Junior Colleges, 3 percent to other institutions, and 2 percent not expecting to enroll in any institution of higher education. Of those eligible for the State Colleges but not for the University of California, approximately 2 percent of the 17 percent eligible plan to enroll in a State College, with another 8 percent planning on going to a Junior College, and 4 percent not planning to enroll at all. And, for the Junior Colleges only half of the 64 percent eligible plan to enroll.

Whatever their reasons, many high school students enroll at public institutions that are lower in presumed quality than those for which they are eligible, with a sizable fraction of high school graduates not enrolling in any public institution whatsoever. Of these latter, however, it must be remembered that some go to private institutions in the state or to colleges outside the state.

TABLE IV-6. ESTIMATED DISTRIBUTION OF PUBLIC SUBSIDIES FOR HIGHER EDUCATION BASED ON AMOUNT RECEIVED DURING PERIOD ENROLLED

	Percentage of Persons Receiving
Amount of Subsidy	
$0	41%
1–749	14
750–1,999	30
2,000–3,499	3
3,500–4,999	3
5,000–6,499	6
6,500 Plus	3
Total	100%

Source: Developed from data in Tables IV-3, IV-4, and IV-5.

DISTRIBUTION OF AMOUNTS OF SUBSIDIES THROUGH HIGHER EDUCATION. We can now construct a rough distribution of the percentage of an age cohort of high school graduates who will receive different amounts of public subsidies for higher education. This is summarized in Table IV-6. The rather startling conclusion is that while a small proportion—9 percent—receives rather large subsidies, exceeding $5,000, more than half of California's young people receive under $750 in total subsidy from higher education. And a substantial portion—41 percent—receive no subsidy at all. This group is divided between those who obtain no higher education whatsoever—almost 80 percent—and those who plan to attend private colleges within California or colleges outside the state— about 20 percent.

In short, there is a highly unequal distribution in the amounts of public subsidies actually received, even though California prides itself on the wide access to higher education it provides and on the high enrollment ratios which are presumably a reflection of this. Moreover, there is little reason to believe that the distribution of public subsidies through higher education is less unequal in other states than it is in California. No state has as widely accessible a junior college system as does California; thus, other states have larger proportions of young people who obtain no college education whatsoever.

DISTRIBUTION OF SUBSIDIES BY FAMILY INCOME. What can be said about the distribution of the subsidies provided through higher education in terms of the students' family income levels? While this is a somewhat more difficult question to answer with the available data, we have been able to restructure one set of data to shed light on this question.

It is useful, to begin with, to gain an idea of the patterns of college-going by level of family income. These are shown in Table IV-7, where columns 3, 4, 5, and 6 show the family income distributions for all California public college students in 1964; column 2 shows the income distribution for families without children in California public higher education; and column 1 shows the distribution for all California families.

The distributions by family income clearly differ among the groups shown. Median family incomes (Table IV-7, bottom row) are highest for parents of University students, followed by State College student families and Junior College student families. Lowest of all is the median for all families without children in the California system. These patterns are about what one might expect and, in general, conform to the patterns shown in other surveys.[7] Thus we conclude that access to subsidies is positively

[7] For example, see the Wisconsin data in L. J. Lins, A. P. Abell, and D. R. Stucki, *Costs of Attendance and Income of Madison Campus Students,*

TABLE IV-7. DISTRIBUTION OF FAMILIES BY INCOME LEVEL AND TYPE OF COLLEGE OR UNIVERSITY, CALIFORNIA, 1964

	All Families	Families Without Children in California Public Higher Education	Families With Children in California Public Higher Education			
			Total	JC	SC	UC
Income Class						
$ 0–3,999	16.1%	17.0%	6.6%	8.1%	4.1%	5.0%
4,000–5,999	14.8	14.9	13.0	15.9	10.2	7.5
6,000–7,999	18.9	19.0	17.6	19.6	17.0	11.1
8,000–9,999	18.1	18.3	16.4	16.9	17.2	13.1
10,000–11,999	12.4	12.1	15.8	14.4	19.9	13.3
12,000–13,999	7.4	7.3	8.8	17.2	10.8	11.3
14,000–19,999	7.9	7.5	13.0	11.1	13.0	20.3
20,000–24,999	1.8	1.6	3.4	2.6	3.3	6.6
25,000 and Over	2.6	2.3	5.4	4.2	4.5	11.8
Total	100.0%	100.0%	100.0%	100.0%	100.0%	100.0%
Median Income	$8,000	$7,900	$9,560	$8,800	$10,000	$12,000

Source: Column 1: Letter from Office of Legislative Analyst, California Legislature, in *Tuition for California's Public Institutions of Higher Education*, Joint Committee on Higher Education Hearings, October 13 and 16, 1967; see Tab T, Table 1. Column 2: Calculated by authors. Column 3: Weighted average of Columns 4, 5, and 6. Columns 4, 5, 6: Edward Sanders and Hans Palmer, *The Financial Barrier to Higher Education in California* (Claremont: Pomona College, 1965), Table M, p. 21, which relates to distribution of parent supported students only.

related to levels of family income, with the highest single year subsidy going to university students (and their families) who already have the highest (median) family incomes ($12,000).[8]

We can present some crude figures to illustrate the association of family income and subsidies received by comparing median family incomes for the groups shown in Table IV-7 with the amounts of the subsidies going to each of these groups. Table IV-8 presents this information, where median income of families of various types is shown in line 1, the one year subsidy received is given in line 2a, and the subsidy as a percentage of family income is presented in line 2b. Because students first enrolling at each type of institution do not remain in college equally long, the average number of years they are enrolled is also shown, in line 3. This information permits calculation of the total subsidy received (line 4a) and of the percentage of family income (line 4b) that the subsidy constitutes. As indicated by line 2b, the values of the single year subsidies vary from zero percent of family income for those without children in public colleges and universities (some of these people may have children in private colleges or in public colleges not in California) to 14 percent of family income for those with State College enrollees. Whereas the average overall subsidy is equal to 9 percent of money income for all parents of publicly enrolled college students (line 2b, column 3), the subsidy climbs to 18 percent of single year family income when we take account of the number of years that the educational subsidy is received (line 4b, column 3). But because, as noted before, the amount of schooling received differs, the average total subsidies (line 4a) rise far more sharply than the single year subsidies, as we contrast the

The University of Wisconsin, 1964–1965 Academic Year (Office of Institutional Studies, January, 1967); I. M. Boyak, A. P. Abell, and L. J. Lins, _Costs of Attendance and Income of University of Wisconsin-Milwaukee Students, 1964–1965 Academic Year_ (Office of Institutional Studies, March, 1967); and L. J. Lins, A. P. Abell, and R. Hammes, _Costs of Attendance and Income of University of Wisconsin Center Students, 1964–1965 Academic Year_ (Office of Institutional Studies, May, 1966).

[8] Were we to relate the data shown in Table IV-7 to the data on subsidies received over the entire college stay, the differences in the subsidies received would be accentuated. The reason is that University of California students are more likely to complete four years than are State College students, and the latter are more likely to complete four years than the vast bulk of the students who begin at Junior Colleges.

TABLE IV-8. AVERAGE FAMILY INCOMES AND
AVERAGE HIGHER EDUCATION SUBSIDIES
RECEIVED BY FAMILIES, BY TYPE OF
INSTITUTION CHILDREN ATTEND,
CALIFORNIA, 1964

	All Families	Families Without Children in California Public Higher Education	Families With Children in California Public Higher Education			
			Total	JC	SC	UC
1. Average Family Income[a]	8,000	7,900	9,560	8,800	10,000	12,000
2. Average Higher Education Subsidy Per Year[b]						
a. Amount in dollars	—	0	880	720	1,400	1,700
b. Percent of Line 1	—	0	9	8	14	13
3. Average Number of Years Higher Education Completed[c]	—	—	1.7	1.2	2.6	2.8
4. Average Total Higher Education Subsidy[c]						
a. Amount in dollars	—	0	1,700	1,050	3,810	4,870
b. Percent of Line 1	—	0	18	12	31	41

[a] Median incomes from Table IV-7.

[b] Average subsidies are based on the distribution of enrollment by year of school and on distribution of enrollment by type of institution.

[c] Average number of years and average subsidies are based on the assumption that entering students progress through the various types of institutions shown in Table IV-4, that students are distributed among the various types of institutions as shown in Table IV-5, and that the various subsidies are those shown in Table IV-3.

families with children enrolled in California Junior Colleges, State Colleges, and University campuses. These patterns of subsidies raise serious questions about the equity of the current system for financing public higher education in California.

At the same time, however, the distributions of students by parental income (as shown by each of the columns in Table IV-7) are so wide for each type of system—University of California, State College, and Junior College—that any strong conclusions about the class-serving nature of the entire system of higher education in California cannot be drawn. While there is a tendency for the higher subsidy schools to draw a higher income clientele, the overlap of the distributions is still very substantial.

Some added light can be thrown on the equity issue by a

TABLE IV-9. DISTRIBUTION OF HIGH SCHOOL GRADUATES BY ELIGIBILITY FOR PUBLIC HIGHER EDUCATION IN CALIFORNIA, BY TYPE OF EDUCATION AND FAMILY INCOME, 1966

| | Percentage Distribution of High School Graduates by Eligibility for | |
	University of California	University of California and State Colleges
Family Income		
$ 0–3,999	10.7%	28.0%
4,000–5,999	11.5	26.3
6,000–7,999	11.9	30.5
8,000–9,999	16.2	33.2
10,000–12,499	19.4	37.1
12,500–14,999	22.5	39.8
15,000–17,499	27.9	45.4
17,500–19,999	29.5	45.1
20,000–24,999	33.3	46.1
25,000 and Over	40.1	54.3
Not Reported	13.3	28.0
All	19.6%	36.3%

Source: Based on data from CCHE, *Financial Assistance Programs,* No. 67-13 (2d rev., October 31, 1967), Table I-2, p. I-9; Table I-3, p. I-10; and Appendix, Table B-3.

Note: Excluded from the sample of 8,162 were 302 students planning vocational training, 38 nonrespondents on enrollment plans, and 20 for whom eligibility was indeterminate.

restructuring of recent data presented by the California Coordinating Council for Higher Education.[9] The data from several of its tables have been combined to show how eligibility and plans for higher education enrollment vary systematically with income.

[9] CCHE, *Financial Assistance Programs,* No. 67-13 (2d rev., October 31, 1967), Table I-2, p. I-9; Table I-3, p. I-10; and Appendix, Table B-3.

We show in Table IV-9 the percentages of all graduating high school seniors eligible to attend the University of California, and the University and the State Colleges. Approximately 80 percent of the high school graduates do not qualify for the substantial University subsidies because of the academic entry requirements. Even more interesting is the fact that the percentage of all students qualifying for the University of California (column 1) rises quite dramatically by family income level—from about 10 percent in the lowest income bracket (under $4,000) to 40 percent in the highest (over $25,000). Thus, the correlation between high school achievement and family income—and all that it reflects—is startling indeed. This pattern persists as we widen our view to include those eligible for both the University and State Colleges (column 2). But a close examination of the differences between the two columns shows that the percentage of those eligible only for the State College system is roughly constant at all income levels; thus, University eligibility requirements account largely for the unequal distribution of opportunity.

The extent to which family income influences the distribution of those *eligible* who *plan* to attend each level of higher education emerges from Table IV-10. For the University (column 1) a larger fraction of upper than lower income students plan to attend; the same holds for the combined University-State College system group (column 2); and the pattern continues—though in somewhat muted fashion—when we consider all high school graduates (column 3). Actually, these results are somewhat deceiving since those eligible for a higher system can attend a lower system. Indeed, when we compare the percent of University eligible students planning to attend one of the three public systems, we find that the proportion is fairly constant with respect to family income, at about 70 to 75 percent (these data are not shown in the accompanying tables). Much the same kind of pattern emerges for both the University and State College eligibles who plan to undertake higher education. The point, however, is that enrollment in a lower system—often dictated by family income considerations—implies a reduced level of subsidies.

WHO PAYS THE TAXES? Having now shown the extent to which families in different income groups are awarded subsidies through the fiscal system by virtue of the provision of higher education, we turn in this section to develop estimates of the state

TABLE IV-10. COLLEGE ATTENDANCE PLANS OF
CALIFORNIA HIGH SCHOOL GRADUATES, BY
FAMILY INCOME AND HIGHER
EDUCATION SEGMENT, 1966

Family Income Level	Percent of UC Eligibles Planning to Attend UC	Percent of UC-SC Eligibles Planning to Attend Either UC or SC	Percent of All California High School Graduates Planning to Attend UC, SC, or JC
$ 0–3,999	30.4%	22.5%	53.1%
4,000–5,999	26.1	29.7	56.1
6,000–7,999	23.4	28.1	56.3
8,000–9,999	21.5	36.5	60.0
10,000–12,499	25.3	32.6	62.0
12,500–14,999	26.2	37.5	64.6
15,000–17,499	26.9	32.1	63.4
17,500–19,999	33.3	45.7	64.2
20,000–24,999	45.4	52.0	68.2
25,000 and Over	46.7	47.8	57.8
No Response	30.5	30.1	47.9

Source: Same as Table IV-9.

taxes alone and the combined state and local taxes that are paid
by families at each income level. The objective is to provide a
basis for comparing the subsidies received with the tax payments
made. Such information is essential in assessing the equity of the
current methods of financing higher education in the state of
California.

Our approach is to estimate the incidence of the most important
state and local taxes by family income level, in order to note the
absolute amount of taxes paid at each income level. We can then
compare this amount with the subsidy received and note any
differences. But we still have no real way of determining how much
of whatever taxes are paid reflect support for higher education,
as against the many other services provided by state and local
governments.

The average amount of taxes paid at each income level as well
as the effective tax rate, for California state taxes alone and for
state and local taxes combined, is shown in Table IV-11. The most

TABLE IV-11. ESTIMATED TAX BURDENS BY
INCOME CLASS, CALIFORNIA, 1965

	State Taxes Only Per Family[a]	Effective State Tax Rate[b]	State and Local Taxes Per Family[c]	Effective State and Local Tax Rate[b]
Adjusted Gross Income Class				
$ 0–3,999	$ 104	5.2%	$ 474	23.7%
4,000–5,999	132	2.6	527	10.5
6,000–7,999	161	2.3	576	8.2
8,000–9,999	221	2.4	696	7.7
10,000–11,999	301	2.7	833	7.6
12,000–13,999	389	3.0	984	7.6
14,000–19,999	539	3.2	1,228	7.2
20,000–24,999	865	3.8	1,758	7.8
25,000 Plus	2,767	5.5	4,093	8.2

Sources: Personal income, sales, cigarette and beverage taxes by income level were obtained from: Letter from Office of Legislative Analyst, State of California, in *Tuition for California's Public Institutions of Higher Education*, Joint Committee on Higher Education, Hearings, October 13 and 16, 1967; see Tab T, Table 1. State gasoline taxes and local property taxes were based on itemized tax deductions reported on state income tax returns, 1965, and summarized in: Franchise Tax Board, *Annual Reports, 1965 and 1966*, Table 13. Local sales taxes were assumed to be distributed in the same manner as state sales taxes above. Since local sales tax revenues in 1965 equaled one-third of state sales tax revenues, this factor was applied to the estimated amount of state sales taxes in each income level.

[a] Personal income, state sales, cigarette, and alcoholic beverage taxes only.

[b] Taxes as a percent of estimated mean income of each income class. The mean of the highest income interval was arbitrarily assumed to be $50,000.

[c] State taxes include: personal income, sales, cigarette, alcoholic beverage, and gasoline taxes. Local taxes include: local sales and property taxes.

important finding is that while the state tax structure (column 2) seems to be somewhat progressive—that is, the effective tax rate rises with income—except in the lowest income classes, the combined state and local tax structure (column 4) is regressive below $8,000 and is essentially proportional above that level.[10]

We return now to our major task of this section which is to compare the amounts of taxes paid with the subsidies received by families with children enrolled in college so that we can observe the extent to which broad groups of families do or do not receive net subsidies through higher education. In making such a comparison we once again remind the reader that this involves com-

[10] The recent changes in the California state income tax structure have increased the overall progressiveness of the state tax structure, but only slightly.

paring *all* taxes with benefits received from higher education *alone*. As shown by Table IV-12, the annual value of higher education

TABLE IV-12. AVERAGE FAMILY INCOMES, AVERAGE HIGHER EDUCATION SUBSIDIES RECEIVED, AND AVERAGE STATE AND LOCAL TAXES PAID BY FAMILIES, BY TYPE OF INSTITUTION CHILDREN ATTEND, CALIFORNIA, 1964

	All Families	Families Without Children in California Public Higher Education	Families With Children in California Public Higher Education			
			Total	JC	SC	UC
1. Average Family Income[a]	$8,000	$7,900	$9,560	$8,800	$10,000	$12,000
2. Average Higher Education Subsidy Per Year[b]	—	0	880	720	1,400	1,700
3. Average Total State and Local Taxes Paid[c]	620	650	740	680	770	910
4. Net Transfer (Line 2—Line 3)	—	−650	+140	+40	+630	+790

[a] From Table IV-7.

[b] From Table IV-8.

[c] Total state and local tax rates from Table IV-11 were applied to the median incomes for families in each column.

subsidies (line 2) received by a family with a single child enrolled in a public college exceeds the total amount (line 3) of all state and local taxes they pay by rather substantial amounts.[11] On an

[11] Because lower income families tend to average somewhat more children, our focus on the distribution of subsidies per *student* may give a biased picture of the subsidy distribution per *family*. Data limitations prevented us from making this alternative set of calculations. It is not clear, however, how the two distributions would compare. On one hand, taking into account the greater number of children in low income families would cause the total subsidy for the average low income family to rise more than for the higher income family. On the other hand, the fact that each child in a higher income family receives a greater average subsidy causes the total subsidy for the average higher income family to rise more than for the families with

overall basis the average higher education subsidy is $880 per year (line 2, column 3), in contrast to total state and local taxes paid of $740 (line 3, column 3); this results in an annual net transfer of $140 from all taxpayers to parents of college students.

But this average conceals wide differences by type of college. For families with a child at one of the State Colleges or one of the University campuses, the net transfers range from $630 to $790 per year. Meanwhile, families without children or with children not enrolled in public institutions of higher education receive no subsidy whatsoever, while they pay an average of $650 in state and local taxes. This is not to suggest that such families should pay no state and local taxes, for some may have benefitted in the past, others may benefit in the future, and still others may have opted for more expensive non-public California higher education. The fact remains, however, that the current method of financing public higher education leads to a sizeable redistribution of income from lower to higher income (compare lines 1 and 4).

This analysis ignores the distribution of benefits from other types of public programs, some of which are explicitly directed to the non-college, low income segment of the population. This means that a broader analysis is needed of the distribution of the benefits from the full range of government programs. The absence of each information does not lessen the significance of the results presented here, namely that the net benefits of one of California's major expenditure programs are received largely by higher income segments of the population.

CONCLUSION

The two analyses of this chapter indicate clearly the general nature of the redistributive effects of the current method of financing public higher education in California. Some low income persons have benefitted handsomely from the availability of publicly sub-

---

lower incomes. The net effect of these offsetting forces is not clear, *a priori*.

In any case, we do not intend to imply that the subsidies per family are more relevant than the subsidies per child. To the contrary, our own normative judgment is that within considerable limits every child is equally deserving of educational opportunity, notwithstanding the number of his brothers and sisters.

sidized higher education. But on the whole, the effect of these subsidies is to promote greater rather than less inequality among people of various social and economic backgrounds by making available substantial subsidies that lower income families are either not eligible for or cannot make use of because of other conditions and constraints associated with their income position.

What we have found to be true in California—an exceedingly unequal distribution of subsidies provided through public higher education—quite probably is even more true for other states. No state has such an extensive system of local Junior Colleges as does California, and for this reason, no state has such a large percentage of its high school graduates going on to public higher education. As a result we can be rather confident that California has a smaller percentage of its young people receiving a zero subsidy than do other states.

To overcome the effects of the present system would require a substantial overhaul of the pricing system in public higher education, a realignment of the tax structure, and/or a broadening of the eligibility base for public expenditure programs. With respect to the latter alternative, eligibility for public subsidies to young people might well be expanded to embrace all young people—not only those who go on to college—including those who opt for alternative ways of expanding their earning power, such as apprenticeship or on-the-job training or even investments in businesses. In any case, it is clear that whatever the degree to which our current higher education programs are rooted in the search for equality of opportunity, the results still leave much to be desired.

Chapter V

AGENDA FOR RESEARCH

Two major difficulties were encountered in carrying out this study. For one—time after time it became clear that questions of fact could not be resolved because the requisite data did not exist. For another—we frequently found that important issues could not be given adequate treatment because the underlying relationships were not well understood. In this chapter we try to indicate what work needs to be done to overcome these barriers.

We focus first on the kinds of *information* that would be most useful in quantifying further the benefits and costs of public higher education in a particular state.

• There are no published state data on the incomes or earnings of people cross-classified by age, sex, and educational attainment. Neither are there data on incomes of people classified by the type of higher education they obtained (e.g., university, state college, junior college, private college, or type of curriculum). The absence of such information makes it difficult to estimate the monetary benefits of higher education and the foregone incomes of students attending college. Although no *current* data on incomes exist, the underlying 1960 Census data could be utilized to provide useful benchmarks; these can be adjusted upward to reflect income shifts since 1960. More important for the future, plans should be developed to make more effective use of the 1970 Census data when they become available.

• Greater effort should be given to assembling information on migration patterns of persons receiving higher education. The extent to which people migrate outside the county in which they were educated (if they attended a locally supported college) and outside the state itself (if they attended a state supported college) deserves exploration.

• More precise and current estimates of capital and instructional costs—both incremental and average—for various types of colleges and by levels within them (lower and upper division, and graduate level) are essential in gaining a better understanding of the total costs of higher education.

• Improved information on patterns of student progress through the various types and levels of public colleges and universities, and patterns of transfer among them, would be helpful in determining the amounts of subsidies various students receive. Particularly interesting would be information on patterns of enrollment, transfer, and progress of students classified by family income levels.

• The preparation of estimates of the responsiveness of enrollments to changes in student charges (the elasticity of demand with respect to tuition) for entire state systems of public higher education as well as for each component of these systems should receive high priority. Only in this way will it be possible to evaluate the impact of changes in student fees and in the level and mix of needed student financial aid.

• The preparation of tabulations showing how much student financial aid goes to students at different family income levels and at different types of schools, as well as how these patterns differ among states, would be helpful in assessing both the efficiency and equity of present student financial aid policies.

• More comprehensive and more precise estimates are needed of the federal, state, and local taxes paid on the added incomes accruing as a result of more education. In addition, information would be useful on the amounts of taxes paid by families with and without children in public higher education, with the families cross-classified by level of income, age, and education of family head. This could be further supplemented by information on the ages of their children and amounts and types of education planned and already attained.

• Efforts should also be made to utilize national sample data available for college educated groups in order to relate their earnings to the types and amounts of higher education they received, and where. Important information on migration patterns might also be obtained as a by-product. In addition, individual states may want to undertake periodic sample surveys of their populations that would permit obtaining basic demographic, social, and economic data. These data would aid in the evaluation of programs in higher education, as well as in other areas.

To deal with all of the quantitative and conceptual problems raised in this chapter will require a substantial amount of both financial and intellectual resources. We have not tried to estimate the amounts of these resources which will be necessary. But, with total expenditures on higher education rising steadily and rapidly it does seem sensible to allocate substantial sums to research in the hope that the results of this research will help lead the way to more effective decision-making in higher education.

While much can be done to augment the small but rapidly growing body of data on the benefits, costs, and finance of higher education, a substantial number of theoretical and conceptual issues remain unresolved. This means that at best only a partial picture of benefits and costs can be presented, whether we focus on California, some other state, or the nation as a whole. We point out some of these issues below.

• The much discussed but little understood concept of the *external effects* from higher education deserves fuller analysis, not only to specify the nature and range of these effects but also to suggest how they can be quantified and, eventually, evaluated in dollar terms. Moreover, since universities often, although not always, produce multiple products, it is important to try to relate external effects to particular functions—teaching, research, public service, and so forth—wherever possible.

• As yet little is known about the *consumption benefits* of higher education. The precise definition of these benefits, their operational measurability, and their quantitative significance all require fuller exploration.

• Certain conceptual problems regarding the wide range of benefits from higher education for *females* are as yet unresolved. Estimation of the monetary benefits is much more complex than it is for males, in part because of the patterns of female labor force participation associated with marriage and child-rearing responsibilities. In addition, more study is required to evaluate the nonmonetary benefits, particularly those having intergenerational effects.

• A comprehensive approach for analyzing the benefits and costs of *graduate education* needs to be developed. We noted earlier the multiple roles of graduate students—as outputs, and as inputs to both undergraduate education and faculty research—which complicate efforts to quantify and allocate both the private and social benefits and costs of their training.

• Much sharper attention should be directed toward deciding what should be meant by *ability to pay* for higher education. To what degree is there a difference between what people feel they can pay and what others say they ought to pay?

• In addition, little is understood concerning the effects on college attendance patterns of offering low cost *loan funds as against outright grants*. More thought must be given to means by which the financial barriers to college attendance can be assessed, and to more effective means for circumventing them.

• Finally, it is important to learn more about the extent to which *efficiency and equity* considerations in higher education policy are in harmony or in conflict. Just as there are real difficulties in specifying the precise meaning of these concepts, much work is required to explore both the possible and the desirable trade-offs among these two goals.

Chapter VI

CONCLUSION

The objective of this study has not been to develop proposals for reform of any state's system of higher education or reform of the methods by which it is financed. Instead, our objective has been to provide background information and a method of analysis to assist in the resolution of those complex issues. More specifically, our goal has been to suggest ways to identify and examine the benefits, costs, and finance of higher education in a state—illustrated by California —to provide estimates of their magnitudes and to indicate the next steps in broadening our knowledge of these matters.

A variety of important and broad policy questions have emerged from this analysis. Although they were discussed in the text, it seems useful to summarize some of them here and to point out their implications for public policy.

• *The limited responsiveness of the California tax system* to changes in income levels will be a continuing source of difficulty with respect to financing public services, among them higher education. Incomes grow through time, but because the California state and local tax system is essentially proportional—that is, tax revenues grow at the same rate as income—while demand for higher education grows at a faster rate, we can forecast, with some confidence, increasing fiscal pressure unless the tax system is made more responsive.

• *Through the local, state, and federal tax systems* many people other than students benefit financially from the increased incomes generally received by college educated persons. But because of the population mobility process, these benefits do not always accrue to the taxing unit that subsidizes the education. These circumstances —both the migration and the presence of a federal tax system which yields a national benefit from each state's expenditure on higher education—provide a justification for increased *federal* support for higher education.

• *Foregone income is a major component of college costs* and deserves fuller recognition as such, particularly for students from low income families. This is the major cost of attending college— not tuition and fees—and is now borne almost entirely by students and their parents. One effective method of recognizing such costs would be to provide substantial grants (negative tuition) to low income youngsters to help offset the high cost to them and their parents of giving up much of their immediate (albeit low) earning capacity.

• *Public subsidies for higher education in California* tend to go disproportionately to students from relatively high income families and are received in quite different amounts by people even within given income classes. Almost 40 percent of the student age population receives no subsidy whatsoever, while a relatively small group receives very substantial subsidies. Whether this pattern of subsidy distribution is consistent with the social objective of equality of educational opportunity is certainly open to question.

• These disparities raise important questions about the *equity of subsidy policies as they affect all young people.* Attention might well be given to a more neutral policy, offering a subsidy even to those youngsters who are unable or unwilling to spend four years attending a college or university. Such a grant might be for participation in a training or apprenticeship program outside the state's higher education system, for investment in a small business, or for some other use which—like higher education—would be regarded as an investment in future income.

• *Choices among alternative systems of financing* public higher education involve a number of dimensions including *which* groups share the cost, *how much* of the cost is borne by each, *when* the students' portion of cost is paid, and the extent to which different students pay different prices for their education. Policy choices in each case produce effects on the amount of resources devoted to public higher education, on their distribution among types of higher education systems and geographic areas, and on the actual utilization of public higher education by various social and economic groups.

This study has disclosed a variety of issues in the higher education area that are important for efficient and equitable decision-making. Some involve concepts, such as consumption benefits, which are understood only superficially. Others, such as mobility patterns of college educated persons, involve data which have simply not been gathered. It is all too easy to call for additional research and for more and better data. Yet the size of the stakes in higher education justify a far more strenuous effort than has been made heretofore to provide the needed research and data.

We conclude with two policy proposals: If equality of opportunity is to be achieved, the subsidy concept must be expanded to embrace a variety of forms of investment in future earning power and not be restricted to formal higher education. It is quite apparent that not all young people either desire to, or are eligible to take advantage of, public higher education. Thus, the limiting case would be to provide a cash subsidy to each young person at age eighteen to use as he sees fit. The desirability of such an approach requires further discussion.

Meanwhile, the following is already clear. The existing system for financing public higher education in California—low (below-cost) student charges, with the balance being made up through state and local tax revenues—is such that Californians who attend public colleges and universities receive considerable benefits. They receive more in the way of direct educational benefits than they and their families pay through the entire state and local tax system during the period of college attendance. Even when the student's entire working lifetime after college is considered, the taxes (income, sales, property, and excise) he pays out of the additional income attributable to his college education fall considerably short, on a present value basis, of the average subsidy he received.

The paradox of the situation is that those who benefit most from the public higher education system are, in general, those least in need of help in paying for what they receive. But by virtue of the structure of California state and local taxes (which are regressive at the lower end and proportional thereafter) and the long-standing policy of below-cost (officially zero) pricing, there is presently no effective device for shifting more of the financial costs of higher education from those who benefit little or are least able to pay to those who derive the most direct monetary benefits or who are most able to pay. Either a change in the state and local tax structure—to make it more progressive—or a change in the system of user charges for higher education—to charge on the basis of ability to pay, and where necessary, to provide generous supplements to low income students—seems called for.

Epilogue

AN OPTIMAL POLICY FOR FINANCING HIGHER EDUCATION—SOME GUIDELINES

The preceding chapters have dealt with means for assessing the costs and benefits of public higher education—from the point of view of any particular state. Now we leave this subject to consider some broader issues in the financing of public higher education. These two subjects are closely related, however, in that the main reason for interest in the magnitudes and distributions of the costs and benefits of public higher education stems from the search by individuals and legislators for a desirable system of educational finance. Thus, although this epilogue—which does stand somewhat independently—could have been omitted from this volume, its inclusion seemed appropriate.

It is not our purpose here to examine the varied educational finance plans that have been put forth, such as income tax credits for college expenses, the Educational Opportunity Bank, or substantial general Federal support for education. These plans have already been explored by others. Nor is it our objective to propose a "best" financing plan. In fact, we do not propose any specific plans. Not that one is not needed, but the state of knowledge simply prevents us from making a precise set of recommendations as to the level or levels of tuition, the appropriate percentage distribution of governmental support (federal, state, and local), and the terms under which loan funds should be available. Making such recommendations requires first identifying and defining—at the *conceptual* level—a desirable finance plan, and second, devising *operational* measures of those concepts. We cannot deal with the second task because of the formidable problems of quantifying the magnitudes of such variables as the external benefits of public higher education, value added by education, and so on. This chapter deals with and indeed is restricted to the first task—the clarification and sharpening of the conceptual issues.

To discover the characteristics of a "best" system for financing public higher education is to find answers to the questions of *who* should bear the costs of public higher education and *how* the portion of costs that is borne by students should be paid. More precisely, the main question of *who* should pay involves determining the share of costs to be paid by students versus taxpayers. (There is, of course, the question of how the taxpayers' portion of the costs is to be shared among various groups, but we do not deal with this matter.)

The question of *how* students should pay relates directly to the tuition issue, but the term tuition is not a simple one. Should tuition be the same for all students? Whatever the level or levels of tuition, should it be paid at the time the education is received or later? Should the level of tuition be determined at the time the education is received, or should the amount be contingent on future benefits? The nature of these choices will be described more fully below. Throughout our analysis we rely heavily on the search for efficient and equitable solutions to these educational finance questions. Indeed, this chapter is divided into two sections, the first focusing on efficiency in the pricing of higher education and the second focusing on equity.

As with this entire study, we continue to direct our attention to decision-making in the public sector. This is somewhat artificial; the fact that there exists a private as well as a public sector in higher education means that success in devising an efficient and equitable finance system for the public sector does not assure either efficiency or equity for the higher education system as a whole. The question of what separate and distinct roles ought to be fulfilled by the public and private sectors in higher education is, in our view, an important one, but scant attention has been given to it. And to deal with the question here would have further complicated an already knotty set of issues.

EFFICIENT PRICING

In this section we discuss efficient pricing from the individual and the social points of view since both are relevant in evaluating alternative methods of financing public higher education.

The cost of a college education to a student and his family—apart from the income foregone—can be analyzed in two parts. One is what can be termed the price of the education—the tuition charge, the books and supplies, and so forth. The second is the ease of financing that price—that is, the availability and terms of loan funds and scholarships.

The level of the price of college education and the ease of financing it are jointly relevant to individuals' decisions. An apparently high tuition rate may be quite manageable if grants or scholarships are widely available or if loans can be obtained at sufficiently low interest rates. Similarly, even a total failure of scholarship programs and capital markets to provide financing assistance can turn out to be inconsequential if the *total* price of education (including foregone income) is sufficiently low. Thus, there would seem to be trade-off possibilities between the price of education and the means of financing it—combinations among which any particular individual would be indifferent.

But considerations of public policy dictate that we go beyond an analysis of any individual's preferences to take account of the resources used up in the process of satisfying those preferences. This involves recognition of a socially efficient price as well as of a socially efficient set of finance terms, including an interest rate.

Efficiency may be said to exist in a market when the price of the good or service is equated with the marginal opportunity cost (value of the best alternative use) of the resources used to produce it, and both are equated with the benefits from an additional unit of the good. Thus, given the distribution of income, the preferences of all individuals in society, and the technological production possibilities, the efficient price for any given unit of production (e.g., year) of higher education is the price which is equal to the marginal *net* social cost of providing that education and to the marginal benefit received by the student. By *net* cost we mean the marginal cost of production *minus* the marginal external benefits (if any), the latter being the externalities noted in Chapter II.[1] These externalities, it may be recalled, consist of the benefits that are not captured by the individuals whose education produced them.

To the extent that such uncaptured external benefits occur, the efficient price of education—to be charged of students—would be below the marginal cost of producing the education services. (It is difficult to estimate marginal costs, but it might reasonably be assumed that long run marginal costs can be approximated by average instructional plus capital costs.) Thus, the likelihood of *under*-investment in education is reduced (though the probability of *over*-investment is increased) as the price confronted by the student and his family is cut via a public subsidy which, at least in principle, is a reflection of the external social benefits from an incremental unit of education.

This view of pricing clearly implies that society (taxpayers in general) should subsidize higher education as a matter of efficiency. Since some external benefits may be realized within local areas while others may be distributed more broadly, all levels of government—federal, state, and local—would presumably share in the costs. Insofar as the bulk of externalities accrue at the national level—in part because of population migration—this would argue for a reallocation of public financing of higher education away from state and local governments and to the federal government.

These subsidies could take any of a variety of forms. One is the obvious and currently prominent low (presumably below-cost) tuition rates. Others include income tax credits or deductions to parents and outright cash grants to students—all of which can be equivalent to a tuition reduction. Any of these forms, and no doubt others as well, could be used to produce the desired public subsidy and, in turn, result in an efficient price. The choice among them rests largely on equity considerations—that is, the extent

---

[1] At the conceptual level, the possibility of external costs as well as benefits should be considered. It is not generally argued, however, that such costs are notable in higher education.

to which persons not in need would benefit. For example, income tax credits would have a negligible effect on low income groups inasmuch as they had little or no income tax liability anyway. Later in this chapter we do discuss broad equity issues, although we regard it as beyond our objective to examine in detail the case for each possible form of subsidy.

EDUCATIONAL CAPITAL MARKETS—PAY NOW OR PAY LATER. Just as there is a socially efficient price for higher education, there is also a socially efficient borrowing rate for those who cannot or prefer not to finance their education from past savings, current income, or family gifts and transfers. The capital market constitutes a device for financing education in a series of installments rather than fully at the time of purchase. But insofar as the capital market for higher education finance reflects a divergence between the private borrowing rate and the social opportunity cost, there will be smaller expenditures for higher education than are optimal.

There is a discrepancy between these two rates because the private risk (to lenders) on loans for education exceeds the social risk—a point which we shall elaborate momentarily. As a result, education loans will tend, in the private market, to be excessively difficult to obtain. For persons whose income and/or asset position is strong, high private borrowing rates will not be a significant barrier to borrowing, for they can utilize collateral other than the prospect of financial gain from education. For the less affluent, however, the difficulty of borrowing to finance the costs of higher education can prove serious. Both equity and efficiency suffer when the market interest rate exceeds the optimal rate. We shall return to equity matters later. Let us now consider efficiency in the loan market in more detail.

Why has there been such a limited development of an organized private capital market to finance student loans for higher education? Several major reasons emerge. Higher education, unlike ordinary commodities, is intangible. A refrigerator, an automobile, or a factory can be repossessed by the mortgage holder in the event of default on a loan. Since education is embodied in the individual, such repossession is impossible in a free society. Thus, given the difficulty of assessing individual integrity and of gaining access to a claim on the borrower's income, the lender's risk in making loans to finance higher education is raised. Higher education is also embodied in a highly mobile form. Because people—especially the better educated—are highly mobile geographically, a private lender finds it risky to finance higher education; subsequent collection is difficult (costly) if the individual moves and especially if he is hard to locate. This situation is in marked contrast with the case of many categories of physical capital which are usually more difficult to move.

There is, in addition, lack of certainty that higher education actually will bring financial benefits for any particular individual. The individual may die prematurely, become disabled, or fail to find regular employment for his skills. These contingencies are analogous to the possibility that a factory will not be profitable because it is destroyed by fire or storm, or because the demand for the product is insufficient. Since some of these events are insurable, it would seem possible to develop an insurance arrangement with respect to the variety of contingencies that might prevent higher education from producing financial benefits for the individual.

However, some reasons for loss may not be easily insurable, inasmuch as a moral hazard may exist. For example, an individual may *choose* a low-paying job over a high-paying one or, particularly in the case of women, may not choose to work for pay at all. Or education may have been acquired solely for consumption purposes or to provide the option of a more attractive, though not necessarily more financially rewarding, job. Again, insurance against these possibilities might be developed but the problem of adverse selection—heavy borrowing by persons who are particularly likely to default—could be serious. This might help to explain the lack of development of private insurance in this area.

Were it not for these special characteristics of the private capital market for higher education loans, there would be no particular reason for concern about whether the price of higher education was paid at the time the education was received or whether it was paid subsequently—just as there is no particular concern about whether business firms finance their investments in plant and equipment in cash or through borrowed funds, or about whether automobile-buying consumers pay in cash or in installments.

An efficient capital market—just as an efficient price—can be achieved in several ways. These include, for example, loan guarantees, interest rate subsidies, and assistance to private lenders in the collection of loans, e.g., through the federal income tax system.

(We shall discuss such possibilities in more detail below.) The effect of these subsidies would be two-fold: First, by reducing the cost of capital to students, some students would be permitted to attend college who otherwise would not; and second, some shift in the method of student financing of college costs would occur, with more of the individuals' costs being shifted to later time periods. It should be pointed out, however, that *any* device that encourages people to go to college by making available to them low cost loans —as distinguished from reduced tuition, increased grants and scholarships, and so forth—will cause more of them to go into debt. This does raise an equity point that we note in passing. Indebtedness in low income families is especially likely to grow. Borrowing by higher income students (or their parents) may grow too, simply because of the attractive interest rates, but these students (or their families) have less basis for concern about their ability to repay. One expected result of interest rate subsidization is, thus, to increase the availability of higher education to low income students, but it does so at the price of burdening them with debts with which their more fortunate colleagues need not be concerned.

It is also important to point out that these subsidies logically would be paid for by the federal government. Efforts by local governments or even states to establish a socially efficient interest rate will not work effectively, particularly in view of national mobility patterns.

We now recapitulate. Assuming the presence of external benefits and the special characteristics of the capital market for college loans, there will exist divergencies between marginal private production costs (to the schools) and net social costs. Prices based on the marginal net social costs of education and interest rates based on the marginal social cost of borrowing to finance such education are requisites for an efficient pricing system in both the higher education and the capital markets. Determination of the appropriate magnitudes for these prices and interest rates remains a matter for further study.

With respect to the interest rate, efficiency in the allocation of resources between higher education and other public and private uses suggests that the appropriate concept for determining the interest rate is the opportunity cost of the funds—that is, the rate of return available on alternative investments. There has been considerable literature dealing with the appropriate rate of interest (or discount) for use in evaluating government expenditure programs, but there is little professional consensus. Recently, however, the Joint Economic Committee of the United States Congress has favored using the private opportunity cost of capital in evaluating all government programs. While no specific figure was recommended, there were references to magnitudes of perhaps 10 percent —a figure which is a rough estimate of the average pretax rate of return on manufacturing capital in the United States. This is not the appropriate place for a discussion of conceptual issues involved in evaluating government expenditure programs. Suffice it to say that discount rates considerably lower than 10 percent are being used in the evaluation of many government expenditure programs —rates as low as 2 percent not being unheard of. Thus, since the opportunity cost of foregoing some projects is 2 percent, while for others it is 10 percent or more, it seems reasonable to settle on a discount rate which falls somewhere in the middle of the range.

If, for example, an interest rate of 5 percent were charged on loans for higher education, it is quite likely that there would be an extremely high demand for such funds, simply because this rate is below that of most market rates confronting individual borrowers today. Thus, such a program would call for setting an upper limit on the amount of the loans so that unlimited borrowing for a wide variety of other purposes could not take place under the guise of financing higher education.

The notion that low interest rate loans are desirable for the financing of higher education is hardly novel, and, in fact, there are already a number of such programs in existence financed by the federal government, state and local governments, and by private groups. It is worth pointing out, though, that one's support for low interest rate loans can be based on considerations of economic efficiency alone, independent of considerations of equity, such as the desire for equality of access to higher education.

Whatever may be the attractiveness of low interest loans, it is not a matter of indifference to state legislators whether the student's share (price) of higher education is paid now or later. There frequently are political and legal constraints on the degree to which the state can borrow in order to finance expenditures, even though repayment (in this case by students) is expected in the future.

A well developed capital market for higher education would

provide a means of coping with this situation. Students and their families could choose between paying the price of higher education out of their own funds or borrowing and repaying in installments; and in either case the state could receive immediate payment. An analogy is the case of an individual buying a new automobile: The automobile dealer (state government) receives cash for the sale either directly from the buyer (student) or indirectly, from the finance company, in the event that the buyer prefers to pay on an installment basis.

CONTINGENT OR FIXED PAYMENT. The opportunity for students to pay for higher education in installments rather than fully at the time the education is received suggests the possibility of making the amount of the payment contingent on some subsequent events, such as the realization of financial benefits from that higher education. Our earlier discussion of the price of education had assumed a *fixed* price, but we now interpret it as an average, expected price —some persons paying more, others less.

A pricing system in which the price is contingent on events occurring subsequent to the date of purchase (transaction) is not new. It is found generally in the insurance field. The total price that an individual pays for a $10,000 ordinary life insurance policy, for example, depends on how long he lives, and the total price that one pays for disability insurance depends on the actual occurrence or lack of occurrence of a disability. Pursuing the life insurance analogy a bit further, it is worth noting that everyone who has such a life insurance policy will eventually collect $10,000, although some individuals will have paid much more than that, and others will have paid much less. The *average* price paid for that $10,000 policy will be approximately $10,000, but the price paid by particular individuals will vary substantially around that average. As with all analogies, that between life insurance and higher education is less than perfect, but our point here is simply to note the practical possibilities for developing a system in which the price actually paid for higher education by a specific individual is not the same *ex post facto* for all individuals and is a function of developments occurring subsequent to the time of purchase of the education.

The above discussion implies that if the pay-now option is selected, the fixed sum would be paid, whereas, if the pay-later option is chosen, either the fixed-sum or variable-sum alternative is available. We judge that as a practical matter this is the case. It is logically possible, however, to utilize the variable-sum alternative regardless of whether the pay-now or pay-later option is selected; the latter would probably require, however, an awkward arrangement of periodic rebates and/or additional payments.

If a variable-sum repayment plan were adopted, the need to define the nature of the variable sum to be repaid would have to be faced. We would argue, on efficiency grounds, for repayment to be based upon the value added by higher education. While value added cannot be comprehensively measured to include both money and non-money returns, money benefits may serve as a reasonable proxy for total benefits. In any case, it is the *additional* benefits (increase in income) directly attributable to a unit of education that are relevant—rather than simply the level of benefits (level of income).

If students and parents are risk averters, a requirement that the price of higher education be fixed independently of the financial benefits actually received will depress purchases of higher education to a level that is suboptimal in terms of expected income gains. Adoption of a pricing system based on incremental income, by contrast, would be more congenial to risk averters, for it would amount to a profit-sharing plan in which taxpayers as a whole shared in the additional productivity (earnings) resulting from higher education. When the additional productivity is small, the bulk of the higher education cost would be borne by taxpayers generally; only when the additional productivity is large would the individual be expected to pay a large fraction of the cost of his education.

One point to note with respect to any plan which bases payments (price) on money income—either on the value added by education or on the absolute level of income—is that higher education provides people with options to choose either higher paying jobs or more pleasant and enjoyable but not so high paying jobs. Thus, a pricing system based only on money income would still have some incentive (efficiency) effects insofar as people were encouraged to reorient their work effort toward jobs producing less money income but more non-money benefits.

Suggestions have been made recently—e.g., the Educational Opportunity Bank proposal—to base charges for higher education on the absolute level of one's subsequent income. This would make the price of education a variable one, but would not relate the price of education to its value-added. Many variables other than schooling also affect incomes; consequently, a pricing system for higher education that makes price simply a function of income level would overprice education relative to its financial benefits for some persons and underprice it for others.

Both the equity and the allocative efficiency of such a pricing system are questionable. While little is known about the quantitative nature of individuals' responses to a pricing system based on one's actual income level rather than on the expected value added, we can analyze the types and directions of the responses.

It would be useful, albeit rather arbitrary, to divide all potential students into two groups: Group A, consisting of those for whom education is an investment in increased earnings, and Group B, consisting of those for whom education is essentially a consumer good. Members of group B—who do not expect a college education to increase their incomes significantly—may be subdivided into group B_1, those (including many women, but also including the lazy and unambitious) who expect relatively *low* incomes whether they go to college or not; and group B_2, those (including some women) who expect *high* incomes whether they go to college or not—simply because they are very able, energetic, hard-working people.

If repayment is to be based upon value added, Groups B_1 and B_2 pay no tax because their education produces no incremental income. But if repayment is based upon *levels* of income, the impact is quite different. Members of Group B_1, whose incomes would be low, would still pay little or nothing. But members of Group B_2, whose incomes would be high—though not as a consequence of their education—would pay much more in taxes. Thus, the consumer-good benefits of higher education would be a bargain for persons in Group B_1, compared with those in Group B_2.

Since the price confronting members of Group B_1 would be lower than under the presently existing pricing system, we could expect an increased amount of higher education to be demanded by them. At the same time, because Group B_1 members would not be paying their own way, members of Groups B_2 and A would be faced with prices (tax payments) greater than under the existing system. Although we do not know the precise nature of the demand function for higher education for each of these three groups, we can be reasonably certain that they are downward sloping (the lower the price, the greater will be the quantity of education demanded). Thus, we can predict an increase in the number of people from Group B_1 taking advantage of the bargain rate and a reduction in the numbers from Groups B_2 and A. We would expect further that some persons from these latter groups would opt for alternatives to college. These alternatives might include on-the-job training, schooling that is the equivalent of college but which goes by some other name, or still other forms of activity which are designed to do essentially what colleges now do; presumably, these could accomplish everything now done by colleges except providing "college" degrees.

We need not dwell on these and other possibilities. Our principal objective has been to examine some consequence of a pricing system that disregards the value added by education. Lest we appear to be advocating a pricing system based only on value added, we hasten to add that the value-added basis for pricing college education also poses serious problems. One is the empirical problem of estimating value added, a matter which was noted above. A second problem is the conceptual issue of whether actual or potential value added should be measured. Actual and potential value added may deviate substantially, especially if only money income is considered; this is particularly true for women not in the labor force and for others who accept lower paying but otherwise more attractive jobs.

A third problem with the value-added approach is that a *market* income measure of either actual or potential value added is incomplete. The value of education as a consumer good is not reflected by money income data.

EQUITY IN HIGHER EDUCATION FINANCE

While the subsidization of the price of education and of the interest rate for college loans can provide an efficient solution to college financing questions, equity considerations must still be treated. Many people who desire to go to college and who would profit from it may still be unable to attend even under socially efficient pricing arrangements. And so we explore methods by which equity objectives can be achieved in order to move closer to the goal of equality of educational opportunity for all.

There are some individuals who may be qualified for college but who will not attend college because the combinations of available price and interest charges are excessive relative to their financial situation and the strength of their desire to attend. The unwillingness to incur these costs is conditioned, however, by various factors including family income and wealth, family size, parental health, etc. At the same time there may be a social determination that these factors ought not to bar college attendance so that needy individuals with the ability and motivation to benefit from college should go.

If compulsion is to be avoided, these barriers to college attendance could be offset in three general ways: Incomes of such students and their families might be supplemented; the price of college education for them could be reduced; the interest rate applicable to their borrowing for college could be lowered.

It might be argued that the judgment that a student should go to college even though family circumstances would lead him not to go represents an implicit social decision that his family's income is too low. Thus, an increase in family income would seem called for. If the objective, however, is to make it possible for this student to attend college at a minimum cost to others, then the approach of giving needy students cash transfers which are not restricted as to use is likely to be inefficient; very substantial transfers might be required before any of the additional money would be used for this student's higher education. A possible variant is to restrict the use of cash grants to higher education. But this alternative may be difficult to implement, since as a practical matter there is no means for preventing some of the grant money from going to families— even some of them with very low incomes—whose children would have gone to college anyway, and who now, having received the grant, will be able to increase their expenditures on other goods and services. Grants to such families are not necessarily undesirable. The point is that the grants are not required to achieve educational objectives, however justified they may be from the point of view of a more general anti-poverty effort.

Consider now the alternatives of reducing the price or interest rate for the needy. If, to begin with, the price and interest rate were set at socially efficient levels, as discussed above, then further reductions would involve distorting the structure of prices. Thus, further reductions would somewhat sacrifice allocative efficiency in order to bring about effects that were deemed more equitable. Such a trade-off of efficiency for equity is by no means unique to higher education, nor is it necessarily undesirable.

In practice each of the three alternatives is bound to fall short of fully realizing equity objectives. Cash subsidies, tuition rate reductions, or reductions in interest rates are all certain to go to some persons other than those whom society specifically wishes to assist, since the needy and deserving are frequently difficult to discern. The result is that subsidies, in any of the three forms discussed, would go to some extent to the wrong people, with taxpayers, some of whom are themselves worthy of help, paying the cost.

Some perspectives on the dimensions of need can be obtained by dividing the population into several different groups. Group I includes those students (and their families) who are willing and able to pay the full long-run marginal cost (which we suggested above might be approximated by average instructional plus capital cost) and the full market interest rate. There is clearly no need to assist this group. Group II includes those who are willing and able to pay the *optimal* (efficient) price and interest rate (not of external benefits), but not the full price or interest rate; a portion of Group II, while willing to pay these costs, can do so only by incurring some hardship. Group III includes those who are willing and able to pay some positive price and interest rate, though less than the optimal levels; some fraction of this group could pay these amounts but only with some hardship. Finally, Group IV includes those people who would need cash grants to cause them to attend college, being unwilling to attend at any combination of a positive price and interest rate. All four groups are defined to include only those deemed "eligible" in terms of aptitude and motivation to attend college.

One of the implications of the structuring of these four groups is that the amount of subsidy required to cause an individual to attend college is a continuous variable with a wide range. Some students will require very substantial subsidies and others none at all in order to provide full equality of opportunity in higher education.

Identifying those who are deserving of additional subsidies to enable them to go to college is a most difficult task. If we assume, however, that the need for higher education subsidies can be estimated in a satisfactory, if rough, manner (perhaps applying the well-defined standards used in student financial aid analysis), then the perplexing question is who should pay for these equity-based subsidies? Taxpayers? Utilization of this source, while having merit, implies that any sum of money that students and their families cannot afford to pay *can* be paid by, and *should* be paid by, taxpayers in general. But when it is borne in mind that taxpayers in general include many quite low income taxpayers, it becomes clear that a shifting of the financial burden from students and their families to taxpayers involves, to some extent, a shift of the burden to families whose incomes and ability to pay may be less than the ability to pay on the part of students and their parents.

This raises a more fundamental issue of the meaning of "ability to pay." Just as standards have been established for determining how much a family can afford to pay for *higher education,* so might standards be established to determine how much a family could afford to pay in *taxes.* If such a study were done, it might well conclude that families of given size, given needs, and with incomes below some specified amount could not afford to pay any taxes at all; nevertheless, we know that many such families are, in fact, actually paying taxes—and that they would be required to pay even more taxes if state support for higher education were increased.

Another source of subsidy funds for the needy is college students and their parents. We noted above that there are some families, particularly in Group I, who are able and willing to pay more than the efficient price of education. If they were charged a higher price, the subsidies required could be obtained outside the tax system. That is, higher income families would pay more tuition, with the extra funds being made available to permit lower payments for low income students. This would amount to the use of classic price discrimination, to charge what the traffic will bear. One might think of the resulting schedule of charges as reflecting a sliding-scale college payment plan, with the possibility of negative charges for the most needy.

There is still a larger issue, touched on in an earlier chapter, concerning the propriety of limiting subsidies to those who choose college rather than some other means of enhancing individual and social well-being. For the many young people not qualified for college or not interested in attending college under any reasonable pricing conditions, there are a variety of other methods by which they can enhance their incomes and future satisfaction and otherwise become effective citizens. Job training and investments in small businesses are only two substitutes to college-going. Whether from the standpoint of achieving equity or efficiency in resource allocation, it would be highly desirable to make these and perhaps other alternatives available to those young people not opting for college. A broadened subsidy program might well be more costly. But, it would at the same time do much to provide greater equality of opportunity for *all* young people, not merely for college students.

The concepts of efficiency in the allocation of resources and equity in the distribution of access to higher education provide useful starting points in the search for a set of operational norms to be used in the pricing and financing of higher education.

Even after the conceptual issues have been fully explored, the thorny problems of measurement still remain. Once agreement is reached on the kinds of information that are needed, however, it should be possible to develop ways to obtain this information. Although the tasks of quantifying such variables as external benefits and value added in education are *substantial,* we are optimistic that progress can be made. Just as over the past decade a real breakthrough has been made in measuring the direct impact of education on earnings and economic growth, we judge that these remaining measurement problems will also yield to a concentrated measurement effort.

We have noted that efficient pricing of higher education involves a number of dimensions, all of which are subject to conscious choice—for example: whether the price (cost) of higher education must be paid at the time the education is received, or whether it can be financed through time; whether the price should be fixed, independent of subsequent income and other factors, or contingent on post-education events; and whether, if the latter approach is adopted, payment should depend on the level of one's income or the increase in that level (the value added by education).

We have pointed out, further, that subsidies of interest rates to facilitate student borrowing can be substituted for lower tuition rates; and that whereas both interest rates and tuition charges can be varied so as to influence who attends college and how much they are burdened financially in the process, neither interest nor tuition charges can be altered without producing side effects on the allocation of resources.

An effort was also made to spell out the alternative means for achieving greater equity in educational finance through cash grants, reduced tuition rates, or reduced interest rates on college loans for the needy. The question of who should pay for these subsidies was also raised. Should it be taxpayers or should it be other students and their families? Finally, the possibility of extending subsidies for college age people to activities other than college attendance was briefly noted.

We embarked on this chapter to see what we, as economists, could say about how public higher education should be financed. Our own assessment is that although we have been able to point out the relevance of a number of concepts—e.g., marginal cost pricing, value-added pricing, external benefits (to persons other than students)—we have been unable to show how those concepts can be made operational. Our frustration in this respect is matched, however, by the firmness of our view that educational finance decisions cannot be made on a more rational basis until economists and other social scientists and educators turn their attention to quantifying these cost and benefit concepts.

Appendix to Chapter II

THE CALCULATION OF THE
PRESENT VALUE OF EARNINGS
DIFFERENTIALS FROM HIGHER EDUCATION

The present value of the financial returns to higher education as shown on line 6 of Table II-3 was developed in the following manner. Median incomes of all United States residents, by age and education, were taken from the 1960 Census of Population (reporting 1959 incomes) and adjusted upward to represent the 1965 earnings of Californians. This upward revision was accomplished by two percentage adjustments, one to reflect the growth of incomes between 1959 and 1965, and the second to recognize the higher level of California incomes relative to national income levels. The adjustments were calculated separately for each sex at each educational level.

The adjustment factors for translating from 1959 national median incomes to 1965 California incomes were as follows:

	Males	*Females*
High School Graduates	1.32	1.14
Some College	1.29	1.29
College Graduate	1.26	1.37

The result of this adjustment is the following set of estimated 1965 earnings for California males by age and education.

TABLE A-1. 1965 ESTIMATED EARNINGS, CALIFORNIA MALES

	Age Group					
Educational Level	*22–24*	*25–29*	*30–34*	*35–44*	*45–54*	*55–64*
High School Graduates	4,615	6,263	7,197	7,719	7,664	7,145
Some College	3,529	6,220	7,811	8,736	8,736	8,025
College Graduates	3,415	6,691	9,280	11,170	11,844	11,132

For females we carry out the same process and achieve a 1965 distribution of estimated earnings for California females.

TABLE A-2a. PRELIMINARY 1965 ESTIMATED EARNINGS, CALIFORNIA FEMALES

	Age Group					
Educational Level	*22–24*	*25–29*	*30–34*	*35–44*	*45–54*	*55–64*
High School Graduates	2,500	2,446	2,489	2,690	2,978	2,661
Some College	2,812	2,980	2,886	3,403	3,884	3,549
College Graduates	3,535	4,987	4,370	5,206	6,247	6,329

To this estimated distribution of females' earnings we make one further adjustment. To make a rough adjustment for the expected greater incidence of part-time work by high school graduate women as compared to college graduate women, we have multiplied the female high school graduate earnings by one and one-third in all age groups. We acknowledge the rough nature of this adjustment. The estimated female earnings on which the returns to higher education have been calculated are, after adjustment:

TABLE A-2b. 1965 ESTIMATED EARNINGS, CALIFORNIA FEMALES

	Age Group					
Educational Level	*22–24*	*25–29*	*30–34*	*35–44*	*45–54*	*55–64*
High School Graduates	3,330	3,260	3,320	3,587	3,971	3,548
Some College	2,812	2,980	2,886	3,403	3,884	3,549
College Graduates	3,535	4,987	4,370	5,206	6,247	6,329

From Tables A-1 and A-2b we calculated the returns from higher education to individuals, to the state of California, and to the federal government. Note that the entries in Tables A-1 and A-2b differ from Table II-2 in four respects: the year to which they apply, 1965; geographical coverage, California only; age span covered, 22–65; the part-time work adjustment, for high school graduate women.

The present value of the earnings differentials which appear in Tables II-3 and II-6 for males and Tables II-7 and II-8 for females are obtained by discounting, at 5 percent, the earnings differentials from Table A-1 and A-2b. Discounting is performed to age eighteen, the age at which the decision to pursue a college education is generally made. Each of the six age groups in Tables A-1 and A-2b is weighted by the number of years to which it applies.

The calculation of the present value of additional state tax collections was done by reducing the present value of ability-adjusted earnings differentials contributed at each age interval by the proportion of individuals no longer living in the state at that age. These mortality-adjusted present values (one for each age interval) were then summed to yield a present value of earnings differentials remaining in the state. The estimated average California state and local tax rate of 10 percent was applied to the present value of remaining earnings differentials to yield a present value of tax collections. Mortality and migration reduction factors were computed for male graduates only. It was assumed that the reduction factors for females would be of a like magnitude and consequently the single set of mortality and migration adjustments was used for males and females, for both college graduates and those with less than four years of college. The calculation of increased federal tax proceeds is unaffected by inter-state migration and results from applying an 18 percent rate to the discounted income differentials.

SELECTED BIBLIOGRAPHY

BOOKS

Becker, Gary S., *Human Capital*. New York: Princeton University Press, 1964.

Blaug, Mark, *Economics of Education: A Selected Annotated Bibliography*. New York: Pergamon Press, 1966.

Campbell, A., and others, *The American Voter*. New York: John Wiley & Sons, Inc., 1960.

Denison, Edward F., *The Sources of Economic Growth*. Washington, D.C.: Committee for Economic Development, 1962.

Journal of Political Economy, Supplement. October, 1962.

Lins, L. Joseph, Abell, Allan P., and Stucki, David R., *Costs of Attendance and Income of Madison Campus Students: The University of Wisconsin, 1964-65 Academic Year*. Madison, Wis.: Office of Institution Studies, University of Wisconsin, January, 1967.

Sanders, Edward, and Palmer, Hans, *The Financial Barriers to Higher Education in California*. Claremont, Calif.: Pomona College, 1965.

Weisbrod, Burton A., *External Benefits of Public Education*. Princeton, N.J.: Princeton University, Industrial Relations Section, 1964.

ARTICLES

Bowman, Mary Jean, "The Costing of Human Resource Development," in E. A. G. Robinson and J. E. Vaizey, eds., *The Economics of Education* (New York: St. Martins, 1966).

Campbell, Robert, and Siegel, B. N., "Demand for Higher Education in the United States." *American Economic Review*, LVII (June, 1967), 482–94.

Hansen, W. Lee, " 'Shortages' and Investment in Health Manpower." *The Economics of Health and Medical Care* (Ann Arbor: University of Michigan, 1964), pp. 75–91.

——, "Total and Private Rates of Return to Investment in Schooling." *Journal of Political Economy*, LXXI (April, 1963), 128–40.

——, and Weisbrod, Burton A., "The Economics of the Military Draft." *Quarterly Journal of Economics*, LXXXI (August, 1967), 395–421.

——, Weisbrod, Burton A., and Scanlon, William J., "Determinants of Earnings: Does Schooling Really Count?" University of Wisconsin, mimeographed, 1968.

Johnson, Harry, "The Economics of the 'Brain Drain': The Canadian Case." *Minerva* (Spring, 1965), pp. 299–312.

Miller, Herman P., "Lifetime Income and Economic Growth." *American Economic Review*, LV (September, 1965), 834–44.

Schultz, T. W., "Capital Formation by Education." *Journal of Political Economy*, LXVIII (December, 1960), 571–83.

Swift, William J., and Weisbrod, Burton A., "On the Monetary Value of Education's Intergenerational Effects." *Journal of Political Economy*, LXXIII (December, 1965), 643–49.

Weisbrod, Burton A., "Education and Investment in Human Capital." *Journal of Political Economy, Supplement* (October, 1962), pp. 106–23.

——, and Karpoff, Peter, "Monetary Returns to College Education." *Review of Economics and Statistics* (November, 1968), pp. 491–97.

Wilkinson, B. W., "Present Values of Lifetime Earnings for Different Occupations." *Journal of Political Economy*, LXXIV (December, 1966), 556–73.

REPORTS AND OTHER MATERIALS

California State Colleges Statement, in *Tuition for California's Public Institutions of Higher Education*. Joint Committee on Higher Education Hearings, October 13 and 16, 1967.

College Entrance Examination Board, *Annual Report on Faculty Salaries, Benefits, and Recruitment,* No. 1023. Sacramento, Calif.: January, 1966.

———, *Feasibility and Desirability of Eliminating Lower Division Program at Selected Campuses of the University of California and the California State Colleges.* Preliminary version, mimeographed, January 6, 1967.

———, *Financial Assistance Programs,* No. 67-13, 2nd rev. October 31, 1967.

———, *The Flow of Students Into, Among, and Through the Public Institutions of Higher Education in California.* Mimeographed, February, 1967.

———, *Student Financial Aid Administration Requirements and Resources at the University of California, 1967,* Vols. I and II, 1967.

Graves, Levern F., "State and Local Tax Burdens in California: The Property Tax Compared with State Taxes," in *Taxation of Property in California,* Part 5. California Legislature, December, 1964.

Total and Full-Time Enrollment: California Institutions of Higher Education, Fall 1965. Sacramento: Department of Finance, undated.

U.S. Bureau of the Census, "Income in 1965 of Families and Persons in the United States," *Current Population Reports,* Series P-60, No. 51. Washington, D.C.: U.S. Government Printing Office, 1967.

INDEX

111